Feminist Contentions

Thinking Gender
Edited by Linda Nicholson

Also published in the series

Feminist
Contentions

A Philosophical Exchange

Seyla Benhabib

Judith Butler

Drucilla Cornell

Nancy Fraser

Introduction by Linda Nicholson

Routledge • New York and London

Published in 1995 by
Routledge
29 West 35th Street
New York, NY 10001

Published in Great Britain by
Routledge
11 New Fetter Lane
London EC4P 4EE

Copyright © 1995 by Routledge

Printed in the United States of America on acid-free paper.

Library of Congress Cataloging-in-Publication Data

Streit um Differenz. English
    Feminist contentions : a philosophical exchange / Seyla Benhabib
. . . [et al.] : with an introduction by Linda Nicholson.
      p.   cm. — (Thinking gender)
    "First published as Der Streit um Differenz (Frankfurt : Fischer Verlag, 1993)" — CIP introd.
    ISBN 0-415-91085-4 : — ISBN 0-415-91086-2 :
    1. Feminist theory.   2. Postmodernism—Social aspects.
I. Benhabib, Seyla. II. Title. III. Series.
HQ1190.S7813   1994
305.42'01—dc20
                                           94-19436
                                              CIP

British Library Cataloging-in-Publication data also available

Contents

A Note on the Text

"Feminism and Postmodernism: An Uneasy Alliance," by Seyla Benhabib; "Contingent Foundations: Feminism and the Question of 'Postmodernism,'" by Judith Butler; and "False Antitheses," by Nancy Fraser were first published in *Praxis International* 11 (2 July 1991). "Subjectivity, Historiography, and Politics," by Seyla Benhabib; "For a Careful Reading," by Judith Butler; "Rethinking the Time of Feminism," by Drucilla Cornell; and "Pragmatism, Feminism, and the Linguistic Turn," by Nancy Fraser were first published in German in *Der Streit um Differenz: Feminismus und Postmoderne in der Gegenwart* (Fischer Taschenbuch Verlag, 1993); they appear here in English for the first time.

Introduction

Linda Nicholson

This volume is a conversation among four women, originating in a symposium organized by the Greater Philadelphia Philosophy Consortium in September 1990. The announced topic was feminism and postmodernism. The original speakers were Seyla Benhabib and Judith Butler with Nancy Fraser as respondent. The selection of this particular group was not accidental. While these three theorists had much in common—a well-established body of writing in feminist theory influenced by past work in continental philosophy—these three were also noted for relating to this topic in different ways. This conjunction of similarity and difference combined with the reputation of each as a powerful theorist seemed to ensure a noteworthy debate. And because that was the consequence, the papers of the symposium were published in the journal *Praxis International* (11:2 July 1991). Following this publication, a decision was made to extend the discussion: to include a contribution from Drucilla Cornell, to have each of the now "gang of four" responding to each other's original paper, and to publish the whole as a book. The volume was first published as *Der Streit um Differenz* (Frankfurt: Fischer Verlag, 1993). This volume marks the appearance of a somewhat altered version of this collection in English.

The above depicts only some of the structural features of this volume; it provides the reader with no sense of its content. But articulating the content of this volume is a particularly challenging task, for reasons best understood through considering a few things the volume is not. For one, this volume is not an anthology on the present state of

1

feminist theory. In 1995, for a collection of essays and responses written by four white women from the United States who come out of a certain tradition within a particular discipline to claim to represent "feminist theory" would represent a kind of arrogance each of these women would vehemently reject. Consequently, this volume makes no claim to provide any kind of overview on contemporary feminist theory. Nor even does it claim to provide a state-of-the-art discussion of "the relationship of feminism and postmodernism." Though the phrase "feminism and postmodernism" was used to advertise the original symposium, disagreement soon emerged over the usefulness of the term "postmodernism" as each differently put forth her views on how the discussion should best be described. Thus, a major source of the difficulty I, as introducer, face in telling you, the reader, "what this volume is about" is that partly defining this discussion are differing views on "what this discussion is about." In this respect, this volume is not like an anthology where the topic has been determined in advance and where each of the contributors is asked to speak on it. But this distinctive feature of this volume, combined with the complexity and richness of the ideas expressed, makes any attempt at abstract characterization of the subject matter of this volume problematic, particularly before you, the reader, have any sense of what the authors themselves are saying. Consequently, before I interject my own perspectives on "what this volume is about," let me first provide some brief summarizations of the initial contributions.

Benhabib responded to the original symposium theme by situating the relation of feminism and postmodernism within broader cultural trends. For Benhabib, the present time is one in which some of the reigning traditions of western culture are being undermined. While Benhabib sees much about these traditions which need to be abandoned, she also views some formulations of this overhaul as eliminating too much. Consequently, a major purpose of her original essay was to separate out that which feminists ought to reject from that which we need to retain. Borrowing from Jane Flax's claims about certain key tenets of postmodernism, Benhabib elaborates this separation in relation to the following three theses: the death of man, the death of history, and the death of metaphysics. Benhabib argues that all of these theses can be articulated in both weak and strong versions. The weak versions offer grounds for feminist support. However, Benhabib claims that in so far as postmodernism has come to be equated with the strong formulations of these theses, it represents that which we ought to reject.

Thus, from her perspective, it is more than appropriate that feminists reject the western philosophical notion of a transcendent subject, a self thematized as universal and consequently as free from any contingencies of difference. Operating under the claim that it was speaking on behalf of such a "universal" subject, the western philosophical tradition articulated conceptions deeply affected by such contingencies. The feminist take on subjectivity which Benhabib supports would thus recognize the deep embeddedness of all subjects within history and culture. Similarly, Benhabib welcomes critiques of those notions of history which lead to the depiction of historical change in unitary and linear modes. It is appropriate that we reject those "grand narratives" of historical change which are monocausal and essentialist. Such narratives effectively suppress the participation of dominated groups in history and of the historical narratives such groups provide. And, finally, Benhabib supports feminist skepticism towards that understanding of philosophy represented under the label of "the metaphysics of presence." While Benhabib believes that here the enemy tends to be an artificially constructed one, she certainly supports the rejection of any notion of philosophy which construes this activity as articulating transcultural norms of substantive content.

But while there are formulations of "the death of man," "the death of history," and "the death of metaphysics" which Benhabib supports, there are also formulations of these theses which she considers dangerous. A strong formulation of "the death of man" eliminates the idea of subjectivity altogether. By so doing, it eliminates those ideals of autonomy, reflexivity, and accountability which are necessary to the idea of historical change. Similarly, Benhabib claims that certain formulations of the death of history negate the idea of emancipation. We cannot replace monocausal and essentialist narratives of history with an attitude towards historical narrative which is merely pragmatic and fallibilistic. Such an attitude emulates the problematic perspectives of "value free" social science; like the latter, it eliminates the ideal of emancipation from social analysis. And, finally, Benhabib rejects that formulation of "the death of metaphysics" which entails the elimination of philosophy. She argues that philosophy provides the means for clarifying and ordering one's normative principles that cannot be obtained merely through the articulation of the norms of one's culture. Her argument here is that since the norms of one's culture may be in conflict, one needs higher-order principles to resolve such conflict. Also, she claims that there will be times when one's own culture will not necessarily provide those norms which are most needed. Philosophy again is necessary to provide that which one's culture cannot.

In general, Benhabib's worry about the strong formulations of these three theses is that they undermine the possibility of *critical* theory, that is, theory which examines present conditions from the perspective of utopian visions. Her belief is that much of what has been articulated under the label of postmodernism ultimately generates a quietistic stance. In short, for Benhabib, certain political/theoretical stances—specifically those which are governed by ideals and which critically analyze the status quo in the light of such ideals—require distinctively philosophical presuppositions, presuppositions which are negated by many formulations of postmodernism.

Judith Butler's concerns, however, are of a very different nature. Butler focuses her attention not on what we need philosophically in order to engage in emancipatory politics, but on the political effects of making claims to the effect that certain philosophical presuppositions *are* required for emancipatory politics. Such a focus reflects her general inclination to inquire about the political effects of the claims that we make and of the questions that we raise. She points to some of the problems involved in the very question: "What is the relation of feminism and postmodernism?" noting that the ontological status of the term "postmodernism" is highly vague; the term functions variously as an historical characterization, a theoretical position, a description of an aesthetic practice and a type of social theory. In light of this vagueness, Butler suggests that we instead ask about the political consequences of using the term: what effects attend its use? And her analysis of such effects are mixed. On the one hand, Butler sees the invocation of the term "postmodernism" as often functioning to group together writers who would not see themselves as so allied. Moreover, many of its invocations appear to accompany a warning about the dangers of problematizing certain claims. Thus, it is frequently used to warn that "the death of the subject" or "the elimination of normative foundations" means the death of politics. But Butler argues: is not the result of such warnings to ensure that opposition to certain claims be construed as nonpolitical? And does not that in turn serve to hide the contingency and specific form of politics embodied in those positions claiming to encompass the very field of politics? Thus, questions about whether "politics stands or falls with the elimination of normative foundations" or "the death of the subject" frequently masks an implicit commitment to a certain kind of politics.

If Butler sees any positive effects of the use of the term "postmodernism,"—and the term she better understands is "poststructuralism" —it is to show how power infuses "the very conceptual apparatus that seeks to negotiate its terms." Here her argument should not be interpreted as a simple rejection of foundations, for she states that "theory posits foundations incessantly, and forms implicit metaphysical commitments as a matter of course, even when it seeks to guard against it." Rather it is against that theoretical move which attempts to cut off from debate the foundations it has laid down and to remove from awareness the exclusions made possible by the establishment of those foundations.

The task then for contemporary social theory committed to strong forms of democracy is to bring into question any discursive move which attempts to place itself beyond question. And one such move Butler draws our attention to is that which asserts the authorial "I" as the bearer of positions and the participant of debate. While not advocating that we merely stop refering to "the subject," she does advocate that we question its use as a taken-for-granted starting point. For in doing so, we lose sight of those exclusionary moves which are effected by *its* use. Particularly, we lose sight of how the subject itself is constituted by the very positions it claims to possess. The counter move here is not merely to understand specific "I's" as situated within history; but more strongly, it is to recognize the very constitution of the "I" as an historical effect. This effect cannot be grasped by that "I" which takes itself as the originator of its action, a position Butler sees as most strikingly exemplified by the posture of the military in the Gulf war. Again, for Butler, the move here is not to reject the idea of the subject nor what it presupposes, such as agency, but rather to question how notions of subjectivity and of agency are used: who, for example, get to become subjects, and what becomes of those excluded from such constructions?

This position, raises, of course, the status of the subject of feminism. Butler looks at the claim that postmodernism threatens the subjectivity of women just when women are attaining subjectivity and questions what the attainment of subjectivity means for the category of "woman" and for the category of the feminist "we." As she asks: "Through what exclusions has the feminist subject been constructed, and how do those excluded domains return to haunt the 'integrity' and 'unity' of the feminist 'we'?" While not questioning the political necessity for feminists to speak as and for women, she argues that if the radical democratic impetus of feminist politics is not to be sacrificed, the category "woman" must be understood as an open site of potential contest. Taking on asserted claims about "the materiality of women's bodies" and "the materiality of sex," as the grounds of the meaning of "woman," she again looks to the political effects of the deployment of such phrases. And employing one of the insights developed by Michel Foucault and Monique Wittig, she notes that one such effect of assuming "the materiality of sex" is accepting that which sex imposes: "a duality and uniformity on bodies in order to maintain reproductive sexuality as a compulsory order."

Thus, the concerns of Benhabib and Butler appear very different. Where Benhabib looks for the philosophical prerequisites to emancipatory politics, Butler questions the political effects of claims which assert such prerequisites. Are there ways in which the concerns of each can be brought together? Nancy Fraser believes that there are. While Fraser's original essay was written as a response to the essays of Benhabib and Butler, one can see in it the articulation of a substantive set of positions on the issues themselves. This is a set of positions which Fraser views as resolving many of the problems which Benhabib and Butler identify with the stance of the other.

Many of Fraser's criticisms of Benhabib's essay revolve around how Benhabib has framed the available options; Fraser claims that the alternatives tend to be articulated too starkly with possible middle grounds overlooked. In relation to "the death of history," Fraser agrees with Benhabib's rejection of the conflict as that between an essentialist, monocausal view of history and one which rejects the idea of history altogether. However, she claims that Benhabib fails to consider a plausible middle-ground position: one which allows for a plurality of narratives, with some as possibly big and, all, of whatever size, as politically engaged. Fraser hypothesizes that Benhabib's refusal to consider such an option stems from Benhabib's belief in the necessity of some metanarrative grounding that engagement. Consequently, conflicts between her position and that of Benhabib's around "the death of history" ultimately reduce to conflicts between the two concerning "the death of metaphysics."

Whereas Benhabib asserts the need for a notion of philosophy going beyond situated social criticism, Fraser, pointing to the position articulated by her and myself in an earlier essay, questions such a need. Fraser claims that the arguments Benhabib advances for such a notion of philosophy are problematic, since the norms Benhabib states are necessary for resolving intrasocial conflict or providing the exile with a means for critiquing her/his society must themselves be socially situated in nature. Consequently, if what is meant by philosophy is an "ahistorical, transcendent discourse claiming to articulate the criteria of validity for all other discourses," then social criticism without philosophy is not only possible, it is all we can aim for.

Whereas it is through criticisms of Benhabib's formulations of the options available around "the death of history" and "the death of metaphysics" that Fraser articulates her own position, it is through criticisms of Butler's formulation of the options available around "the death of the subject" that Fraser's ideas on this topic come forth. She agrees with Butler that to make the strong claim that subjects are constituted, not merely situated, is not necessarily to deny the idea of the subject as capable of critique. However, Fraser believes that there are aspects of Butler's language, particularly, her preference for the term "re-signification" in lieu of "critique," which eliminates the means for differentiating positive from negative change. Fraser sees the need for such differentiation in relation to several positions she views Butler as adopting from Foucault: that the constitution of the subjectivity of some entails the exclusion of others, that resignification is good and that foundationalist theories of subjectivity are inherently oppressive. As Fraser questions: "But is it really the case that no one can become the subject of speech without others being silenced? ... Is subject-authorization *inherently* a zero-sum game?" She notes that foundationalist theories of subjectivity—such as the one of Toussaint de l'Ouverture—can sometimes have emancipatory effects. Fraser believes that being able to differentiate the positive from negative effects of re-signification, processes of subjectification and of foundationalist theories of subjectivity requires the adoption of those critical-theoretical considerations which she views as absent from the kind of Foucauldian framework Butler adopts. Finally, Fraser believes that introducing these kinds of consideration would enable Butler to advance a more elaborated conception of liberation than is present in Butler's discussion of feminist politics.

Fraser's essay was developed as a response to the papers of Benhabib and Butler, as was demanded by the structure of the initial symposium. Drucilla Cornell's essay, contributed after the symposium had taken place, is more of an independent articulation of her own position. Like Butler, Cornell questions the need for foundationalist principles. Instead, Cornell advocates that feminists adopt what she describes as the ethical attitude, a stance that aims for a nonviolent relationship to the Other, which includes the Other within oneself. She notes that such an attitude has much in common with what Charles Peirce has described as fallibilism and musement, that is "an openness to challenge of one's basic organization of the world" and "the stance of amazement before the mysteries and marvels of life that takes nothing for granted." Like Butler, Cornell does not view this attitude as entailing a negation of principles. Instead she views it as representing a negation of the idea of fixed or ultimate principles.

Cornell views the ethical attitude as particularly central to the feminist project. She sees the reigning system of gender hierarchy generating fantasies of Woman which deny difference other than that enacted in its divide between the "good" and "bad" girl. For Cornell, the feminist project is made possible by the discrepany between the diverse lived realities of women and the totalities which the fantasies construct. Thus, any claimed feminist project which speaks in the name of totality must represent merely another incarnation of the reigning fantasies.

Cornell elaborates these ideas through a reading of Lacan modified by Derrida. Lacan offers the insight that the category of "Woman" which operates within the realm of the symbolic cannot be fixed in relation to any ultimate ground of biology or of role. In short, there is for Lacan "no fixed signified for Woman within the masculine symbolic." For Cornell, this insight provides us with an understanding of the transformative possibility of feminism. Because there is "no fixed signified for Woman within the masculine symbolic," feminism can assert difference within the meaning of "Woman" against those tropes which deny it. Secondly, Cornell takes from Lacan the claim that the denial of the feminine within sexual difference serves as the ground of culture. Unlike those psychoanalytic narratives which situate the father and the child's relationship to him as central to ego formation, Lacanian theory's focus on the castrated Mother makes the issue of the resymbolization of the feminine the key to the overthrow of that which has been taken for "civilization."

However, within the narrative offered by Lacanian theory, such a resymbolization is impossible. Women, whose signification within this story of psychic development is that of "lack," can escape from the split image of good girl/bad girl presented to them only by attempting to appropriate the phallus, that is, by entering the boys' club. A representation of feminism which attempts a resignification of the feminine is ruled out. While Cornell sees much in this analysis which is helpful for explaining the difficulties feminism faces—i.e. that feminism *will* persistently encounter the move to place it on the side of the masculine—she also sees weaknesses in the theory whose correction would overcome the hopeless conclusion it generates.

Specifically, Cornell sees weaknesses in Lacan's claim that the bar to the resignation of the feminine is absolute. The bar is certainly there, which is why for Cornell, feminism is not easy. But, drawing on the work of Derrida and Wittgenstein, she notes that there is greater possibility of slippage in the signification of Woman than Lacan allows. We make possible such resignification in the act of mimetic identification as we expose the gap between the fantasies and images of Woman allowed to us and the complexities of the lives we lead.

The Questions From Here

But what now shall we say is the relation among these claims? How shall we describe the points of conflict and of these which shall we say are merely the products of misunderstanding and which shall we state represent genuine and interesting theoretical differences? There are no easy answers to these questions, as how one describes the issues of conflict and which one depicts as serious and interesting must in part depend on one's own theoretical stance. This phenomenon emerges in the responses where each author poses the differences between her own position and those of each of the others in complex ways. Rather than attempting to summarize these complexities, I would instead like to focus on certain themes which *I* see as interesting in the responses. From these themes I derive certain questions which I believe would move the discussion forward.

One productive conflict I identify in the responses is that between Seyla Benhabib and Judith Butler around the issues of subjectivity and agency. As noted, Benhabib argued in her initial essay that Butler's position seems to disallow agency, that Butler's discussion of subject constitution suggests a very determinist approach. Benhabib elaborates this argument in her response by claiming that the way out of such determinism must involve some theoretical explanation of how agency becomes possible. And Benhabib claims that accounts which merely describe the historical processes of meaning constitution will not suffice. Also required are explanations of the development of ontogenetic processes, that is explanations which elaborate the structural processes of individual socialization.

The question that I would like to pose to Benhabib is the following: What precisely do we need an account of the "structural processes of individual socialization" to do? Do we need such accounts because the processes by which individuals appear to assume subjectivity from infancy to adulthood appear different from the processes by which subjectivity is attained by groups across history? But if this is the case, that demand appears satisfiable merely by the development of different kinds of narratives of meaning constitution. But I sense that this would not suffice. Implicit in Benhabib's demand seems the idea that there are processes involved in the attainment of individual subjectivity which are independent of historically specific, social interpretations. For that reason, accounts of the attainment of individual subjectivity must be different *in kind* from accounts which tell us how diverse groups have attained subjectivity across history. But, given the diversity in the ways in which societies seem to understand the relationship between childhood and adulthood, it is not clear to me that those accounts are so different in kind. In short, while I would agree with Benhabib that we do need theoretical explanations of how agency becomes possible, I am not sure why any of these need necessarily be of an "ontogenetic" or transcultural nature.

Benhabib's claim that Butler's discussion of subject constitution needs supplementation by some account of the "structural processes of individual socialization" gains part of its force, I believe, from certain ambiguities in Butler's own remarks, ambiguities whose clarification would undermine the force of such a claim. Benhabib asks the question: "How can one be constituted by discourse without being determined by it?" She goes on to say that "the theory of performativity, even if Butler would like to distinguish gender-constitution from self-constitution, still presupposes a remarkably determinist view of individuation and socialization processes which fall short, when compared with currently available social scientific reflections of the subject." Sometimes Butler appears to respond to such remarks by appealing to features of language, by noting, for example, that as the performative aspect of language constitutes subjects, so it also *re*constitutes or resignifies that which had been constituted and in such resignification agency lies. Thus Butler notes that in *Gender Trouble* she suggested "that change and alteration is part of the very process of 'performativity.'" Also, she states, "In this sense, discourse is the horizon of agency, but also, performativity is to be rethought as resignification." A problem I have with this kind of appeal is that it provides no means to distinguish or explain those instances of performativity which generate new kinds of significations from those which are merely repetitions of previous performative acts. But, there do seem times over the course of the history of societies that change appears more pronounced than at others. Moreover, over the course of individual lives, there also seem times—at least within contemporary cultures that I am familiar with—that change of a certain self-initiated nature appears more pronounced. Given the apparent poverty of a theory of language to account for changes of either kind, the need for other kinds of explanation emerges. Thus, in relation to the inability of a theory of language to account for such changes in individual lives, Benhabib can claim the necessity for other such theories, such as that of socialization.

But there are many other instances in Butler's response that indicate that she does not in fact limit her account of agency to what a theory of language can provide. Butler frequently invokes the need to pay attention to specific historical contexts to explain the possibility of agency. For example, in speaking about gender performativity, she notes that deriving agency from the very power regimes which constitute us is *historical* work. Also, in opposing transcendental notions of the self, she notes that asking the question "what are the concrete conditions under which agency becomes possible" is "a very different question than the metaphysical one. . . ." What these latter remarks suggest to me is that for Butler it is not discourse or performativity per se which operate as "the horizon of agency" but rather certain kinds of discourse or certain kinds of performative acts. From my own perspective, the advantage of the latter appeal is not only that it enables us to distinguish those performative acts which function as repetitions from those which function as transformations, but that it also moves us to distinguish the conditions which support one as opposed to the other. In short, it enables one to respond to Benhabib's justified demand for accounts of the possibility of agency, not with the claim that one does not need such accounts, but rather with the claim that one needs many. On such grounds, existing theories of socialization tend to be impoverished in so far as they too frequently assume that one is enough.

In short, I see Butler as employing two different kinds of responses to Benhabib's objection; clarifying the relation of these responses to each other would undermine the force of the objection. And I see the need for a similar clarification in relation to one of the questions which Fraser asks Butler. As earlier noted, Fraser, in her first essay, questions Butler as to whether subject constitution always produces at least some negative effects. I see the justification for this question in that Butler sometimes appears to attribute a certain inherent negativity to the exclusionary processes of subject constitution. For example, Butler, in her first essay, in arguing that subjects are constituted through exclusion, uses the example that certain qualifications must be met for one to be a claimant in sex discrimination or rape cases. Following the description of this example, Butler then states: "Here it becomes quite urgent to ask, who qualifies as a "who," what systematic structures of disempowerment make it impossible for certain injured parties to invoke the "I" effectively within a court of law?" I read this conjunction of statements to suggest that it is the exclusion itself, and not the effects of this specific exclusion within a certain context, which generates the importance of asking such questions. Similarly, shortly following these remarks she points approvingly to a clarification of Joan Scott that "once it is understood that subjects are formed through exclusionary operations, it becomes politically necessary to trace the operations of that construction and erasure." But this also seems to imply that it is the exclusionary operations per se which make the political questions appropriate.

Butler responds to Fraser's question in the following way. She states that she is misunderstood if she is taken as claiming that the exclusionary processes by which subjects are constructed are necessarily bad. Rather, for her, "the exclusionary formation of the 'subject' is neither good nor bad, but, rather a psychoanalytic premise which one might usefully employ in the service of a political critique." In addition, she states: "My argument is that 'critique,' to use Fraser's terms, always takes place *immanent* to the regime of discourse/power whose claims it seeks to adjudicate, which is to say that the practice of 'critique' is implicated in the very power-relations it seeks to adjudicate." I interpret these remarks to mean that for Butler, issues of good or bad are not appropriately about the construction of subjectivity per se but are immanent to specific discursive regimes. Consequently questions of politics are questions about the construction of specific subjects and the specific exclusions generated by their construction.

I find this clarification of Butler's position helpful in that it locates the grounds of critique within specific historical contexts. However, some questions remain for me—particularly in reference to how Butler thinks about the relation between narratives of psychoanalysis and other types of narratives. For one, it seems inadequate to both say that "the exclusionary formation of the 'subject' is neither good nor bad, . . ." and also to say that one might "usefully employ [it] in the service of a political critique." If it is neither good nor bad, how can one employ it in the service of political critique? What one can employ in the service of a political critique appear only some of the consequences of the exclusionary formation of the subject and these only for reasons which are external to the exclusionary process per se.

Secondly, I want to know more precisely what it is about the exclusionary formation of the subject which makes it neither good nor bad. The way Butler formulated her response suggests that its status as a psychoanalytic phenomenon accounts for this normative neutrality. But my guess is that there are other psychoanalytic phenomena which Butler would want to describe as bad. For example, in the following passage, Butler describes in what appears to be negative terms the psychoanalytic phenomenon of "a disavowed dependency."

> In a sense, the subject is constituted through an exclusion and differentiation, perhaps a repression, that is subsequently concealed, covered over, by the effect of autonomy. In this sense, autonomy is the logical consequence of a disavowed dependency, which is to say that the autonomous subject can maintain the illusion of its autonomy insofar as it covers over the break out of which it is constituted. This dependency and this break are already social relations, ones which precede and condition the formation of the subject. As a result, this is not a relation in which the subject finds itself, as one of the relations that forms its situation. The subject is constructed through acts of differentiation that distinguish the subject from its constitutive outside, a domain of abjected alterity conventionally associated with the feminine, but clearly not exclusively.... There is no ontologically intact reflexivity to the subject which is then placed within a cultural context; that cultural context, as it were, is already there as the disarticulated process of that subject's production, one that is concealed by the frame that would situate a ready-made subject in an external web of cultural relations.

This passage generates questions for me about the relation of the process of subject constitution and that of a disavowed dependency. Are these separable processes? If not, how can we use the latter as the basis of critique as Butler seems to do in her discussion of the stance of the military in the Gulf war? If so, why is it that one psychoanalytic premise can be described as neither good nor bad but the other not? Is it because one, but not the other, is more historically limited and thus more apparently amenable to change? But what then accounts for the emergence of that which is more historically limited?

I raise these questions primarily because I see many of the more general issues they raise as central to much current feminist theoretical debate. Trying to figure out how we conceptualize the relationship between narratives of psychoanalysis and of language—often thought to transcend history and critique—from narratives of more specific historical duration, is not just Judith Butler's problem but seems a problem for many of us. It lies at the heart of many conflicts within contemporary feminist debate, including, in this volume, the debate between Fraser and Cornell.

At the core of Fraser's critique of Cornell is the charge that Cornell is locating the possibility of change within properties of language, i.e., that Cornell is deriving from Derrida's ideas about language the possibility for change not derivable from Lacan. But, Fraser claims, this kind of a derivation will not work, for in Derrida "'what shifts' is posited as a transcendental property of language operating beneath the apparently stable symbolic order. . . . It is not a conception that can theorize actually existing cultural contestation among competing significations that are on a par with one another."

Cornell's response to Fraser involves, for one, a stress on the importance of a psychoanalytic perspective within feminism, that "unconscious motivation and the construction of social fantasy must be the basis of any critical social research program." Also, she argues that her critical appropriation of Lacan cannot be understood as foundational since it asserts the lack of grounding for Woman within the masculine symbolic. As she claims: "My reinterpretation of the impossibility of Woman does not bind us to the logic of phallogocentrism as Fraser suggests. Instead it opens up endless possibilities for the reelaboration of sexual difference."

I, however, do not interpret Fraser as claiming that Cornell is operating with a foundational conception of Woman. Rather, I understand Fraser as saying that Cornell is operating with an ahistorical conception, that is, one which, in Cornell's terms, ahistorically theorizes "the endless possibilities for the reelaboration of sexual difference." Or, to put this criticism in my own terms, what Cornell's account does not seem to provide is an explanation which tells us whether "the unleasing of the feminine imaginary" was equally possible for, say, seventeenth-century India as it is for the twentieth-century United States. In short, the problem that I see Fraser as identifying is that the psychoanalytic and theories of language that Cornell is drawing on are about such an indefinite stretch of history—specified only as "patriarchy"—that they provide no means to theorize the differences within the openness of "Woman" across that stretch. Of note here is that the language Cornell draws upon to elaborate her reinterpretation of Lacan, such as "a feminine symbolic" or "the feminine imaginary" also seems questionably generalizing not only in its use of the articles "a" and "the," but that the term "feminine" itself seems appropriately applicable only to a post late nineteenth century Western context.

None of this denies the validity of Cornell's insistence that we need psychoanalytic theories. We need accounts of the ways in which human symbolization does not operate in coherent ways, and of how fantasy organizes social life. We must also keep in mind the issues about history that Cornell cites from Joan Scott, issues which underline for me the point that there is no objective history out there which can be thought of as a court of last resort. The historical narratives we tell are rooted in our psychic needs. But given all this, the question that still remains in my mind—and here I return to a question I originally posed of Benhabib—is why do we assume that the narratives we tell about our psyches have to be homogeneous among us or assumed to be singular for all contexts where some element of male dominance is present? To borrow from some of Butler's remarks on the concept of universality, the telling of such homogeneous tales has been so implicated in ethnocentric and exclusionary moves that the only way we might now distance ourselves from such moves might be to put the burden of justification on the bigger rather than the smaller story. Clearly, I am advocating here no rules with simple application, only a suspicion that the move which will encourage accounts which are formed from a variety of voices is today also that which will be more hesitant about tall tales than academic theory has tended to be.

• • •

The above reflects only a few of the interesting points of difference in this discussion, i.e., those that *I* identify *as* points of difference and also as interesting. The authors, themselves, offer other
perspectives. I invite you, therefore, to turn your attention to the following essays and responses to form your own assessment "on what
this volume is about."

1

Feminism and Postmodernism: An Uneasy Alliance

Seyla Benhabib

I. The Feminist Alliance With Postmodernism

A decade ago a question haunted feminist theorists who had participated in the experiences of the New Left and who had come to feminism after an initial engagement with varieties of twentieth-century Marxist theory: whether Marxism and feminism were reconcilable, or whether their alliance could end only in an "unhappy marriage"?[1] Today with Marxist theory world-wide on the retreat, feminists are no longer preoccupied with saving their unhappy union. Instead it is a new alliance, or misalliance—depending on one's perspective—that has proved more seductive.

Viewed from within the intellectual and academic culture of western capitalist democracies, feminism and postmodernism have emerged as two leading currents of our time. They have discovered their affinities in the struggle against the grand narratives of Western Enlightenment and modernity. Feminism and postmodernism are thus often mentioned as if their current union was a foregone conclusion; yet certain characterizations of postmodernism should make us rather ask "feminism *or* postmodernism?" At issue, of course, are not merely terminological quibbles. Both feminism and postmodernism are not merely descriptive categories: they are constitutive and evaluative terms, informing and helping define the very practices which they attempt to describe. As categories of the present, they project modes of thinking about the future and evaluating the past. Let us begin then by considering one of the recent more comprehensive characterizations of the "postmodern moment" provided by a feminist theorist.

In her recent book, *Thinking Fragments: Psychoanalysis, Feminism and Postmodernism in the Contemporary West*, Jane Flax characterizes the postmodern position as subscription to the theses of the death of Man, of History and of Metaphysics.[2]

— The Death of Man. "Postmodernists wish to destroy," she writes, "all essentialist conceptions of human being or nature. . . . In fact Man is a social, historical, or linguistic artifact, not a noumenal or transcendental Being. . . . Man is forever caught in the web of fictive meaning, in chains of signification, in which the subject is merely another position in language."[3]

— The Death of History. "The idea that History exists for or is his Being is more than just another precondition and justification for the fiction of Man. This idea also supports and underlies the concept of Progress, which is itself such an important part of Man's story. . . . Such an idea of Man and History privileges and presupposes the value of unity, homogeneity, totality, closure, and identity."[4]

— The Death of Metaphysics. According to postmodernists, "Western metaphysics has been under the spell of the 'metaphysics of presence' at least since Plato. . . . For postmodernists this quest for the Real conceals most Western philosophers' desire, which is to master the world once and for all by enclosing it within an illusory but absolute system they believe represents or corresponds to a unitary Being beyond history, particularity and change. . . . Just as the Real is the ground of Truth, so too philosophy as the privileged representative of the Real and interrogator of truth claims must play a 'foundational' role in all 'positive knowledge'."[5]

This clear and cogent characterization of the postmodernist position enables us to see why feminists find in this critique of the ideals of Western rationalism and the Enlightenment more than a congenial ally. Feminist versions of the three theses concerning the Death of Man, History, and Metaphysics can be articulated.

— The feminist counterpoint to the postmodernist theme of "the Death of Man" can be named the "Demystification of the Male Subject of Reason." Whereas postmodernists situate "Man," or the sovereign subject of the theoretical and practical reason of the tradition, in contingent, historically changing, and culturally variable social, linguistic, and discursive practices, feminists claim that "gender," and the various practices contributing to its constitution, is one of the most crucial contexts in which to situate the purportedly neutral and universal subject of reason.[6] The western philosophical tradition articulates the deep structures of the experiences and consciousness of a self which it claims to be representative for humans as such. But in its deepest categories western philosophy obliterates differences of gender as these shape and structure the experience and subjectivity of the self. Western reason posits itself as the discourse of the one self-identical subject, thereby blinding us to and in fact delegitimizing the presence of otherness and difference which do not fit into its categories. From Plato over Descartes to Kant and Hegel western philosophy thematizes the story of the male subject of reason.

— The feminist counterpoint to the "Death of History" would be the "Engendering of Historical Narrative." If the subject of the western intellectual tradition has usually been the white, propertied, Christian, male head of household, then History as hitherto recorded and narrated has been "his story." Furthermore, the various philosophies of history which have dominated since the Enlightenment have forced historical narrative into unity, homogeneity, and linearity, with the consequence that fragmentation, heterogeneity, and above all the varying pace of different temporalities as experienced by different groups have been obliterated.[7] We need only remember Hegel's quip that Africa has no history.[8] Until very recently neither did women have their own history, their own narrative with different categories of periodization and with different structural regularities.

— The feminist counterpoint to the "Death of Metaphysics" would be "Feminist Skepticism toward the Claims of Transcendent Reason." If the subject of reason is not a supra-historical and context-transcendent being, but the theoretical and practical creations and activities of this subject bear in every instance the marks of the context out of which they emerge, then the subject of philosophy is inevitably embroiled with knowledge-governing interests which mark and direct its activities. For feminist theory, the most important "knowledge-guiding interest" in Habermas's terms, or disciplinary matrix of truth and power in Foucault's terms, is gender relations and the social, economic, political and symbolic constitution of gender differences among human beings.[9]

Despite this "elective affinity" between feminism and postmodernism, however, each of the three theses enumerated above can be interpreted to permit if not contradictory then at least radically divergent theoretical strategies. And for feminists, which set of theoretical claims they adopt as their own cannot be a matter of indifference. As Linda Alcoff has recently observed, feminist theory is undergoing a profound identity crisis at the moment.[10] The postmodernist position(s) thought through to their conclusions may eliminate not only the specificity of feminist theory but place in question the very emancipatory ideals of the women's movements altogether.

II. Feminist Skepticism Toward Postmodernism

Let us begin by considering the thesis of the "Death of Man" for a closer understanding of the conceptual option(s) allowed by the postmodernist position(s). The weak version of this thesis would situate the subject in the context of various social, linguistic, and discursive practices. This view, however, would by no means question the desirability and theoretical necessity of articulating a more adequate, less deluded, and less mystified vision of subjectivity. The traditional attributes of the philosophical subject of the West, like self-reflexivity, the capacity for acting on principles, rational accountability for one's actions and the ability to project a life-plan into the future, in short some form of autonomy and rationality, could then be reformulated by taking account of the radical situatedness of the subject.

The strong version of the thesis of the "Death of the Man" is perhaps best captured in Flax's own phrase that "Man is forever caught in the web of fictive meaning, in chains of signification, *in which the subject is merely another position in language.*" The subject thus dissolves into the chain of significations of which it was supposed to be the initiator. Along with this dissolution of the subject into yet "another position in language" disappear of course concepts of intentionality, accountability, self-reflexivity, and autonomy. The subject that is but another position in language can no longer master and create that distance between itself and the chain of significations in which it is immersed such that it can reflect upon them and creatively alter them.

The strong version of the "Death of the Subject" thesis is not compatible with the goals of feminism.[11] Surely, a subjectivity that would not be structured by language, by narrative and by the symbolic structures of narrative available in a culture is unthinkable. We tell of who we are, of the "I" that we are by means of a narrative. "I was born on such and such a date, as the daughter of such and such . . ." etc. These narratives are deeply colored and structured by the codes of expectable and understandable biographies and identities in our cultures. We can concede all that, but nevertheless we must still argue that we are not merely extensions of our histories, that vis-à-vis our own stories we are in the position of author and character at once. The situated and gendered subject is heteronomously determined but still strives toward autonomy. I want to ask how in fact the very project of female emancipation would even be thinkable without such a regulative principle on agency, autonomy, and selfhood?

Feminist appropriations of Nietzsche on this question, therefore, can only lead to self-incoherence. Judith Butler, for example, wants to extend the limits of reflexivity in thinking about the self beyond the dichotomy of "sex" and "gender." "Gender," she writes "is not to culture as sex is to nature; gender is also the discursive/cultural means by which "sexed nature" or a "natural sex" is produced and established as "prediscursive," prior to culture, a politically neutral surface *on which* culture acts."[12] For Butler, we might say, the myth of the already sexed body is the epistemological equivalent of the myth of the given: just as the given can be identified only within a discursive framework, so too it is the culturally available codes of gender that "sexualize" a body and that construct the directionality of that body's desire.

Butler also maintains that to think beyond the univocity and dualisms of gender categories, we must bid farewell to the "doer beyond the deed," to the self as the subject of a life-narrative. "In an application that Nietzsche himself would not have anticipated or condoned, we might state as a corollary: There is no gender identity behind the expressions of gender; that identity is performatively constituted by the very 'expressions' that are said to be its results."[13] If this view of the self is adopted, is there any possibility of changing those "expressions" which constitute us? If we are no more than the sum total of the gendered expressions we perform, is there ever any chance to stop the performance for a while, to pull the curtain down, and let it rise only if one can have a say in the production of the play itself? Isn't this what the struggle over gender is all about? Surely we can criticize the supremacy of presuppositions of identity politics and challenge the supremacy of heterosexist and dualist positions in the women's movement. Yet is such a challenge only thinkable via a complete debunking of any concepts of selfhood, agency, and autonomy? What follows from this Nietzschean position is a vision of the self as a masquerading performer, except of course we are now asked to believe that there is no self behind the mask. Given how fragile and tenuous women's sense of selfhood is in many cases, how much of a hit and miss affair their struggles for autonomy are, this reduction of female agency to a "doing without the doer" at best appears to me to be making a virtue out of necessity.[14]

Consider now the thesis of "the Death of History." Of all positions normally associated with postmodernism, this particular one appears to me to be the least problematical. Disillusionment with the ideals of progress, awareness of the atrocities committed in this century in the name technological and economic progress, the political and moral bankruptcy of the natural sciences which put themselves in the service of the forces of human and planetary destruction—these are the shared sentiments of our century. Intellectuals and philosophers in the twentieth century are to be distinguished from one another less as being friends and opponents of the belief in progress but more in terms of the following: whether the farewell from the "metanarratives of the Enlightenment" can be exercised in terms of a continuing belief in the power of rational reflection or whether this farewell is itself seen as but a prelude to a departure from such reflection.

Interpreted as a weak thesis, the Death of History could mean two things: theoretically, this could be understood as a call to end the practice of "grand narratives" which are essentialist and monocausal. Politically the end of such grand narratives would mean rejecting the hegemonial claims of any group or organization to "represent" the forces of history, to be moving with such forces, or to be acting in their name. The critique of the various totalitarian and totalizing movements of our century from national socialism and fascism to orthodox Marxism and other forms of nationalisms is certainly one of the most formative political experiences of postmodernist intellectuals like Lyotard, Foucault, and Derrida.[15] This is also what makes the death of history thesis interpreted as the end of "grand narratives" so attractive to feminist theorists. Nancy Fraser and Linda Nicholson write, for example: ". . . the practice of feminist politics in the 1980s has generated a new set of pressures which have worked against metanarratives. In recent years, poor and working-class women, women of color, and lesbians have finally won a wider hearing for their objections to feminist theories which fail to illuminate their lives and address their problems. They have exposed the earlier quasi-metanarratives, with their assumptions of universal female dependence and confinement to the domestic sphere, as false extrapolations from the experience of the white, middle-class, heterosexual women who dominated the beginnings of the second wave ... Thus, as the class, sexual, racial, and ethnic awareness of the movement has altered, so has the preferred conception of theory. It has become clear that quasi-metanarratives hamper rather than promote sisterhood, since they elide differences among women and among the forms of sexism to which different women are differentially subject."[16]

The strong version of the thesis of the "Death of History" would imply, however, a prima facie rejection of any historical narrative that concerns itself with the *longue durée* and that focuses on macro- rather than on micro-social practices. Nicholson and Fraser also warn against this "nominalist" tendency in Lyotard's work.[17] I agree with them that it would be a mistake to interpret the death of "grand narratives" as sanctioning in the future local stories as opposed to global history. The more difficult question suggested by the strong thesis of the "death of history" appears to me to be different: even while we dispense with grand narratives, how can we rethink the relationship between politics and historical memory? Is it possible for struggling groups not to interpret history in light of a moral-political imperative, namely, the imperative of the future interest in emancipation? Think for a moment of the way in which feminist historians in the last two decades have not only discovered women and their hitherto invisible lives and work, but of the manner in which they have also revalorized and taught us to see with different eyes such traditionally female and previously denigrated activities like gossip, quilt-making, and even forms of typically female sickness like headaches, hysteria, and taking to bed during menstruation.[18] In this process of the "feminist transvaluation of values" our present interest in women's strategies of survival and historical resistance has led us to imbue these activities, which were wholly uninteresting from the standpoint of the traditional historian, with new meaning and significance.

While it is no longer possible or desirable to produce "grand narratives of history, the "death of history" thesis occludes the epistemological interest in history and in historical narrative which accompany the aspirations of all struggling historical actors. Once this "interest" in recovering the lives and struggles of those "losers" and "victims" of history is lost, can we produce engaged feminist theory? I remain skeptical that the call to a "postmodern-feminist theory" that would be pragmatic and fallibilistic, that "would take its method and categories to the specific task at hand, using multiple categories when appropriate and foreswearing the metaphysical comfort of a single feminist method or feminist epistemology"[19] would also be a call toward an emancipatory appropriation of past narratives. What would distinguish this type of fallibilistic pragmatics of feminist theory from the usual self-understanding of empirical and value-free social science? Can feminist theory be postmodernist and still retain an interest in emancipation?[20]

Finally, let me articulate strong and weak versions of the "death of metaphysics" thesis. In considering this point it would be important to note right at the outset that much of the postmodernist critique of western metaphysics itself proceeds under the spell of a metanarrative, namely, the narrative first articulated by Heidegger and then developed by Derrida that "Western metaphysics has been under the spell of the 'metaphysics of presence' at least since Plato . . ." This characterization of the philosophical tradition allows postmodernists the rhetorical advantage of presenting what they are arguing against in its most simple-minded and least defensive versions. Listen again to Flax's words: "For postmodernists this quest for the Real conceals the philosophers' desire, which is to master the world" or "Just as the Real is the ground of Truth, so too philosophy as the privilege representative of the Real . . ." etc. But is the philosophical tradition so monolithic and so essentialist as postmodernists would like to claim? Would not even Hobbes shudder at the suggestion that the "Real is the ground of Truth"? What would Kant say when confronted with the claim that "philosophy is the privileged representation of the Real"? Would not Hegel consider the view that concepts and language are one sphere and the "Real" yet another merely a version of a naive correspondence theory of truth which the chapter on "Sense Certainty" in the *Phenomenology of Spirit* eloquently dispensed with? In its strong version the "death of metaphysics" thesis not only subscribes to a grandiose metanarrative, but more significantly, this grandiose metanarrative flattens out the history of modern philosophy and the competing conceptual schemes it contains to the point of unrecognizability. Once this history is rendered unrecognizable, then the conceptual and philosophical problems involved in this proclamation of the "death of metaphysics" can be neglected.

The version of the "death of metaphysics" thesis which is today more influential than the Heidegger-Derrida tall tale about the "metaphysics of presence" is Richard Rorty's account. In *Philosophy and the Mirror of Nature* Rorty has shown in a subtle and convincing manner that empiricist as well as rationalist projects in the modern period presupposed that philosophy, in contradistinction from the developing natural sciences in this period, could articulate the basis of validity of right knowledge and correct action. Rorty names this the project of "epistemology";[21] this is the view that philosophy is a meta-discourse of legitimation, articulating the criteria of validity presupposed by all other discourses. Once it ceases to be a discourse of justification, philosophy loses its *raison d'être*. This is indeed the crux of the matter. Once we have detranscendentalized, contextualized, historicized, genderized the subject of knowledge, the context of inquiry, and even the methods of justification, what remains of philosophy?[22] Does not philosophy become a form of genealogical critique of regimes of discourse and power as they succeed each other in their endless historical monotony? Or maybe philosophy becomes a form of thick cultural narration of the sort that hitherto only poets had provided us with? Or maybe all that remains of philosophy is a form of sociology of knowledge, which instead of investigating the conditions of the validity of knowledge and action, investigates the empirical conditions under which communities of interpretation generate such validity claims?

Why is this question concerning the identity and future and maybe the possibility of philosophy of interest to feminists? Can feminist theory not flourish without getting embroiled in the arcane debates about the end or transformation of philosophy? The inclination of the majority of feminist theorists at the present is to argue that we can side-step this question; even if we do not want to ignore it, we must not be committed to answer it one way or another. Fraser and Nicholson ask: "How can we conceive a version of criticism without philosophy which is robust enough to handle the tough job of analyzing sexism in all its endless variety and monotonous similarity?"[23] My answer is that we cannot, and it is this which makes me doubt that as feminists we can adopt postmodernism as a theoretical ally. Social criticism without philosophy is not possible, and without social criticism the project of a feminist theory, which is committed at once to knowledge and to the emancipatory interests of women is inconceivable. Sabina Lovibond has articulated the dilemma of postmodernists quite well:

I think we have reason to be wary, not only of the unqualified Nietzschean vision of an end of legitimation, but also of the suggestion that it would somehow be "better" if legitimation exercises were carried out in a self-consciously parochial spirit. For if feminism aspires to be something more than a reformist movement, then it is bound sooner or later to find itself calling the parish boundaries into question.

. . .

So postmodernism seems to face a dilemma: either it can concede the necessity, in terms of the aims of feminism, of "turning the world upside down" in the way just outlined—thereby opening a door once again to the Enlightenment idea of a total reconstruction of society on rational lines; or it can dogmatically reaffirm the arguments already marshalled against that idea—thereby licensing the cynical thought that, here as elsewhere, "who will do what to whom under the new pluralism is depressingly predictable."[24]

Faced with this objection, the answer of postmodernists committed both to the project of social criticism and to the thesis of the death of philosophy as a metanarrative of legitimation will be that the "local narratives," "*les petits récits*," which constitute our everyday social practices or language-games, are themselves reflexive and self-critical enough to pass judgments on themselves. The Enlightenment fiction of philosophical reflection, of *episteme* juxtaposed to the noncritical practice of everyday *doxa*, is precisely that, a fiction of legitimation which ignores that everyday practices and traditions also have their own criteria of legitimation and criticism. The question then would be, if among the criteria made available to us by various practices, language games, and cultural traditions we could not find some which would serve feminists in their task of social criticism and radical political transformation.[25] Following Michael Walzer, such postmodernists might wish to maintain that the view of the social critic is never "the view from nowhere," but always the view of the one situated somewhere, in some culture, society and tradition.[26]

I should now like to consider this objection.

III. Feminism as Situated Criticism

The obvious answer to any defender of the view of "situated criticism" is that cultures, societies and traditions are not monolithic; univocal and homogenous fields of meaning. However one wishes to characterize the relevant context to which one is appealing, for example as "the Anglo-American liberal tradition of thought," "the tradition of progressive and interventionist jurisprudence," "the Judeo-Christian tradition," "the culture of the West," "the legacy of the Suffragettes," "the tradition of courtly love," "Old Testament views of justice," "the political culture of democratic welfare states," etc., all these characterizations are themselves "ideal types" in some Weberian sense. They are constructed out of the tapestry of meaning and interpretation which constitutes the horizon of our social lifeworld. The social critic does not find criteria of legitimation and self-criticism to be given in the culture as one might find, say, apples on a tree and goldfish in an aquarium; she no less than social actors is in the position of constantly interpreting, appropriating, reconstructing and constituting the norms, principles, and values which are an aspect of the lifeworld. There is never a single set of constitutive criteria to appeal to in characterizing complex social practices. Complex social practices, like constitutional traditions, ethical and political views, religious beliefs, scientific institutions are not like games of chess. The social critic cannot assume that when she turns to an immanent analysis and characterization of these practices, she will find a single set of criteria on which there is such universal consensus that one can simply assume that by juxtaposing these criteria to the actual carrying out of the practice one has accomplished the task of immanent social criticism. So the first defect of situated criticism is a kind of "hermeneutic monism of meaning," the assumption namely that the narratives of our culture are so univocal and uncontroversial that in appealing to them one could simply be exempt from the task of evaluative, ideal-typical reconstruction.[27] Social criticism needs philosophy precisely because the narratives of our cultures are so conflictual and irreconcilable that, even when one appeals to them, a certain ordering of one's normative priorities and a clarification of those principles in the name of which one speaks is unavoidable.

The second defect of "situated criticism" is to assume that the constitutive norms of a given culture, society, and tradition will be sufficient to enable one to exercise criticism in the name of a desirable future. There certainly may be times when one's own culture, society and tradition are so reified, dominated by such brutal forces, when debate and conversation are so dried up or simply made so impossible that the social critic becomes the social exile. Not only social critics in modernity, from Thoreau to the Frankfurt School, from Albert Camus to the dissidents of Eastern Europe, have exemplified this gesture. Antiquity as well as Middle Ages have had philosophers in exile, chiliastic sects, mystical brotherhoods and sisterhoods, and prophets who have abandoned their cities. Certainly the social critic need not be the social exile; however, insofar as criticism presupposes a necessary distantiation of oneself from one's everyday certitudes, maybe eventually to return to them and to reaffirm them at a higher level of analysis and justification, to this extent the vocation of the social critic is more like the vocation of the social exile and the expatriate than the vocation of the one who never left home, who never had to challenge the certitude of her own way of life. And to leave home is not to end up nowhere; it is to occupy a space outside the walls of the city, in a host country, in a different social reality. Is this not in effect the quintessential postmodern condition in the twentieth century? Maybe the nostalgia for situated criticism is itself a nostalgia for home, for the certitudes of one's own culture and society in a world in which no tradition, no culture, and no society can exist any more without interaction and collaboration, confrontation and exchange. When cultures and societies clash, where do we stand as feminists, as social critics and political activists?

Are we then closer to resolving the question posed at the end of the previous section as to whether feminist social criticism without philosophy was possible? In considering the postmodernists' thesis of the "death of metaphysics," I suggested that the weak version of this thesis proceeded from a rhetorical construction of the history of philosophy as "a metaphysics of presence," while the strong version of the thesis would eliminate, I argued, not only metanarratives of legitimation but the practice of legitimation and criticism altogether. The postmodernist could then respond that this need not be the case, and that there were internal criteria of legitimation and criticism in our culture which the social critic could turn to such that social criticism without philosophy would be possible. I am now arguing that the practice of immanent social criticism or situated social criticism has two defects: first, the turn to immanent or internal criteria of legitimation appears to exempt one from the task of philosophical justification only because the postmodernists assume, *inter alia*, that there is one obvious set of such criteria to appeal to. But if cultures and traditions are more like competing sets of narratives and incoherent tapestries of meaning, then the social critic must herself construct out of these conflictual and incoherent accounts the set of criteria in the name of which she speaks. The "hermeneutic monism of meaning" brings no exemption from the responsibility of normative justification.

In the second place I have argued that the vocation of social criticism might require social exile, for there might be times when the immanent norms and values of a culture are so reified, dead, or petrified that one can no longer speak in their name. The social critic who is in exile does not adopt the "view from nowhere" but the "view from outside the walls of the city," wherever those walls and those boundaries might be. It may indeed be no coincidence that from Hypatia to Diotima to Olympe de Gouges and to Rosa Luxemburg, the vocation of the feminist thinker and critic has led her to leave home and the city walls.

IV. Feminism and the Postmodernist Retreat from Utopia

In the previous sections of this paper I have disagreed with the view of some feminist theorists that feminism and postmodernism are conceptual and political allies. A certain version of postmodernism is not only incompatible with but would undermine the very possibility of feminism as the theoretical articulation of the emancipatory aspirations of women. This undermining occurs because in its strong version postmodernism is committed to three theses: the death of man, understood as the death of the autonomous, self-reflective subject, capable of acting on principle; the death of history, understood as the severance of the epistemic interest in history of struggling groups in constructing their past narratives; the death of metaphysics, understood as the impossibility of criticizing or legitimizing institutions, practices, and traditions other than through the immanent appeal to the self-legitimation of "small narratives." Interpreted thus, postmodernism undermines the feminist commitment to women's agency and sense of selfhood, to the reappropriation of women's own history in the name of an emancipated future, and to the exercise of radical social criticism which uncovers gender "in all its endless variety and monotonous similarity."

I dare suggest in these concluding considerations that postmodernism has produced a "retreat from utopia" within feminism. By "utopia" I do not mean the modernist understanding of this term as the wholesale restructuring of our social and political universe according to some rationally worked-out plan. These utopias of the Enlightenment have not only ceased to convince but with the self-initiated exit of previously existing "socialist utopias" from their state of grace, one of the greatest rationalist utopias of mankind, the utopia of a rationally planned economy leading to human emancipation, has come to an end. The end of these rationalistic visions of social engineering cannot dry up the sources of utopia in humanity. As for the longing for the "wholly other" (*das ganz Andere*), for that which is not yet, such utopian thinking is a practical-moral imperative. Without such a regulative principle of hope, not only morality but also radical transformation is unthinkable. What scares the opponents of utopia, like Lyotard for example, is that in the name of such future utopias the present in its multiple ambiguity, plurality, and contradiction will be reduced to a flat grand narrative. I share Lyotard's concerns insofar as utopian thinking becomes an excuse either for the crassest instrumentalism in the present—the end justifies the means—or to the extent that the coming utopia exempts the undemocratic and authoritarian practices of the present from critique. Yet we cannot deal with these political concerns by rejecting the ethical impulse of utopia but only by articulating the normative principles of democratic action and organization in the present. Will the postmodernists join us in this task or will they be content with singing the swan song of normative thinking in general?

The retreat from utopia within feminist theory in the last decade has taken the form of debunking as essentialist any attempt to formulate a feminist ethic, a feminist politics, a feminist concept of autonomy, and even a feminist aesthetic. The fact that the views of Gilligan or Chodorow or Sarah Ruddick (or for that matter Kristeva) articulate only the sensitivities of white, middle-class, affluent, first-world, heterosexual women may be true (although I even have empirical doubts about this). Yet what are we ready to offer in their place? As a project of an ethics which should guide us in the future are we able to offer a better vision than the synthesis of autonomous justice thinking and empathetic care? As a vision of the autonomous personality to aspire to in the future are we able to articulate a sense of self better than the model of autonomous individuality with fluid ego-boundaries and not threatened by otherness?[28] As a vision of feminist politics are we able to articulate a better model for the future than a radically democratic polity which also furthers the values of ecology, nonmilitarism, and solidarity of peoples? Postmodernism can teach us the theoretical and political traps of why utopias and foundational thinking can go wrong, but it should not lead to a retreat from utopia altogether. For we, as women, have much to lose by giving up the utopian hope in the wholly other.[29]

Notes

To republish an essay which was first written in 1990, and which has since appeared in various forms in other places, requires some justification. I am persuaded by the argument that to make this controversy available in its original form to a wider-reading public is significant. This exchange brought four of us who share profound ties of personal friendship into open public disagreement about our theoretical and political commitments. This process has not always been easy: public disagreements have strained personal loyalties and friendships. Nonetheless, serious intellectual exchanges are processes through which the life of the mind and the community of scholarship is enhanced. And as is to be expected from a deep controversy, no one has remained untouched by its consequences. For my own part, I am continuing to pursue the complex issues raised by this debate as they touch upon human subjectivity, agency, historiography, and politics in a new manuscript called *Alice Doesn't Live Here Anymore. Feminism and the Problem of the Subject.*

1. See Lydia Sargent, ed., *Women and Revolution: A Discussion of the Unhappy Marriage of Marxism and Feminism* (Boston: South End Press, 1981).

2. Jane Flax, *Thinking Fragments: Psychoanalysis, Feminism and Postmodernism in the Contemporary West* (Berkeley: University of California Press, 1990), 32 ff.

3. *Ibid.*, 32.

4. *Ibid.*, 33.

5. *Ibid.*, 34.

6. Luce Irigaray, *Speculum of the Other Woman*, trans. by Gillian C. Gill (Ithaca: Cornell University Press, 1985), 133 ff.; Genevieve Lloyd, *The Man of Reason. Male and Female Western Philosophy* (Minneapolis: University of Minnesota Press, 1984); Sandra Harding and M. Hintikka, eds. *Discovering Reality. Feminist Perspectives on Epistemology, Metaphysics, Methodology and Philosophy of Science* (Dordrecht: Reidel Publishers, 1983).

7. Joan Kelly Gadol, "The Social Relations of the Sexes: Methodological Implications of Women's History," and "Did Women Have a Renaissance?" in: *Women, History and Theory* (Chicago: University of Chicago Press, 1984), 1–19 and 19–51.

8. G. W. F. Hegel, "At this point we leave Africa not to mention it again. For it is no historical part of the world: it has no movement or

development to exhibit. Historical movements in it—that is in the northern part—belong to the Asiatic or European World . . . What we properly understand by Africa, is the Unhistorical, Undeveloped Spirit, still involved in the conditions of mere nature . . . " in: *The Philosophy of History*, trans. by J. Sibree and Introd. by C. J. Friedrich (New York: Dover Publications, 1956), 99.

9. For a provocative utilization of a Foucauldian framework for gender analysis, cf. Judith Butler, *Gender Trouble. Feminism and the Subversion of Identity* (New York and London: Routledge, 1990).

10. Linda Alcoff, "Poststructuralism and Cultural Feminism," *Signs* Vol. 13, No. 3 (1988) 4-5-36 and Christine di Stefano, "Dilemmas of Difference: Feminism, Modernity, and Postmodernism, in: *Feminism/Postmodernism*, Linda Nicholson, ed. (London and New York: Routledge, 1990), 63–83.

11. See Rosi Braidotti, "Patterns of Dissonance: Women and/in Philosophy," in: *Feministische Philosophie*, ed. by Herta Nagl-Docekal (Vienna and Munich: R. Oldenburg, 1990), 108–23; Herta Nagl-Docekal, "Antigones Trauer und der Tod des Subjekts." Lecture held at the "Philosophinnen-Ringvorlesung at the Institute of Philosophy," Freie Universität Berlin, on May 25, 1990.

12. Butler, *Gender Trouble*, 7.

13. *Ibid.*, 25.

14. Rosi Braidotti remarks very appropriately: "It seems to me that contemporary philosophical discussions on the death of the knowing subject, dispersion, multiplicity, etc. etc. have the immediate effect of concealing and undermining the attempts of women to find a theoretical voice of their own. Dismissing the notion of the subject at the very historical moment when women are beinning to have access to it, while at the same time advocating the *"devenir femme"* (as Guattari does, S.B.) of philosophical discourse itself, can at least be described as a paradox. . . . The truth of the matter is: one cannot de-sexualize a sexuality one has never had; in order to deconstruct the subject one must first have gained the right to speak as one; before they can subvert the signs, women must learn to use them; in order to de-mystify meta-discourse one must first have access to a place of enunciation. *"Il faut, au moins, un sujet."* in: "Patterns of Dissonance: Women and/in Philosophy," in: *Feministische Philosophie*, Herta Nagl-Docekal, ed. 119–20.

15. Cf. Vincent Descombes, *Modern French Philosophy* (New York: Cambridge University Press, 1980).

16. Nancy Fraser and Linda J. Nicholson, "Social Criticism Without Philosophy: An Encounter Between Feminism and Postmodernism," in: *Feminism/Postmodernism*, ed. by Linda Nicholson, 33. Iris Young makes the same point in her "The Ideal of Community and the Politics of Difference," in the same volume, 300–1.

17. *Ibid.*, 34.

18. The pioneering anthology in different languages in this respect is: *Becoming Visible. Women in European History*, ed. by R. Bridenthal, C. Koonz, and S. Stuard (Boston: Houghton Mifflin Co., 1987).

19. *Ibid.*, 35.

20. For an interesting, even if acrimonious, exchange on the question of agency in history and how different views might influence social and historical research, see Joan W. Scott's Review of "Heroes of their Own Lives: The Politics and History of Family Violence" by Linda Gordon; Linda Gordon's review of "Gender and the Politics of History" by Joan Scott and their Responses, in: *Signs*, Vol. 15, No. 4 (Summer 1990), 848–60.

21. Richard Rorty, *Philosophy and the Mirror of Nature* (Princeton: Princeton University Press, 1979), 131 ff.

22. For trenchant accounts of the various problems and issues involved in this "sublation" and "transformation" of philosophy, see *After Philosophy. End or Transformation?*, ed. by Kenneth Baynes, James Bohman, and Thomas McCarthy (Cambridge, Mass.: MIT Press, 1987).

23. Fraser and Nicholson. "Social Criticism Without Philosophy," 34.

24. Sabina Lovibond, "Feminism and Postmodernism," in: *New Left Review*, No. 178 (November–December 1989), 5–28; here 22.

25. See Lyotard's remark, "narratives . . . thus define what has the right to be said and done in the culture in question, and since they are themselves a part of the culture, they are legitimated by the simple fact that they do what they do." in: *The Postmodern Condition: A Report on Knowledge*, trans. Geoff Bennington and Brian Massumi (Minneapolis: University of Minnesota Press, 1984), 23. In his intervention in this debate, Rorty has sided with Lyotard and against Habermas, maintaining that the latter "scratches where it does not itch." Cf. R. Rorty, "Habermas and Lyotard on Postmodernity," *Praxis International*, Vol. 4, No. 1 (April 1984), 34. I have analyzed the difficulties of this turn to immanent social criticism in "Epistemologies of Postmodernism: A Rejoinder to Jean-Francois Lyotard," reprinted in: Nicholson, ed. *Feminism/Postmodernism*, 107–130.

26. See Michael Walzer, *Interpretation and Social Criticism* (Cambridge: Harvard University Press, 1987), especially 8–18.

27. See Georgia Warnke's discussion of Michael Walzer's position for an alternative account more sympathetic to the possibility of immanent, social criticism than my own, "Social Interpretation and Political Theory: Walzer and His Critics," in: *The Philosophical Forum*, Vol. xxi, Nos. 1–2 (Fall–Winter 1989–90), 204 ff.

28. Jessica Benjamin, *The Bonds of Love: Psychoanalysis, Feminism, and the Problem of Domination* (New York: Pantheon Books, 1968).

29. For a feminist position which seeks to retain this utopian element even while affirming postmodernist philosophy, see Drucilla Cornell, "Post-structuralism, the Ethical Relation, and the Law", *Cardozo Law Review*, Vol. 9, No. 6, 1587–1628 and "From the Lighthouse: The Promise of Redemption and the Possibility of Legal Interpretation," *Cardozo Law Review*, Volume 11, Nos. 5–6 (July–August 1990), pp. 1687–1714.

2

Contingent Foundations: Feminism and the Question of "Postmodernism"

Judith Butler

The question of postmodernism is surely a question, for is there, after all, something called postmodernism? Is it an historical characterization, a certain kind of theoretical position, and what does it mean for a term that has described a certain aesthetic practice now to apply to social theory and to feminist social and political theory in particular? Who are these postmodernists? Is this a name that one takes on for oneself, or is it more often a name that one is called if and when one offers a critique of the subject, a discursive analysis, or questions the integrity or coherence of totalizing social descriptions?

I know the term from the way it is used, and it usually appears on my horizon embedded in the following critical formulations: "if discourse is all there is. . . ," or "if everything is a text. . . ," or "if the subject is dead. . . ," or "if real bodies do not exist. . . ." The sentence begins as a warning against an impending nihilism, for if the conjured content of these series of conditional clauses proves to be true, then, and there is always a then, some set of dangerous consequences will surely follow. So "postmodernism" appears to be articulated in the form of a fearful conditional or sometimes in the form of paternalistic disdain toward that which is youthful and irrational. Against this postmodernism, there is an effort to shore up the primary premises, to establish in advance that any theory of politics requires a subject, needs from the start to presume its subject, the referentiality of language, the integrity of the institutional descriptions it provides. For politics is unthinkable without a foundation, without these premises. But do these claims seek to secure a contingent formation of politics that requires that these notions remain unproblematized features of its own definition? Is it the case that all politics, and feminist politics in particular, is unthinkable without these prized premises? Or is it rather that a specific version of politics is shown in its contingency once those premises are problematically thematized?

To claim that politics requires a stable subject is to claim that there can be no *political* opposition to that claim. Indeed, that claim implies that a critique of the subject cannot be a politically informed critique but, rather, an act which puts into jeopardy politics as such. To require the subject means to foreclose the domain of the political, and that foreclosure, installed analytically as an essential feature of the political, enforces the boundaries of the domain of the political in such a way that that enforcement is protected from political scrutiny. The act which unilaterally establishes the domain of the political functions, then, is an authoritarian ruse by which political contest over the status of the subject is summarily silenced.[1]

To refuse to assume, that is, to require a notion of the subject from the start is not the same as negating or dispensing with such a notion altogether; on the contrary, it is to ask after the process of its construction and the political meaning and consequentiality of taking the subject as a requirement or presupposition of theory. But have we arrived yet at a notion of postmodernism?

A number of positions are ascribed to postmodernism, as if it were the kind of thing that could be the bearer of a set of positions: Discourse is all there is, as if discourse were some kind of monistic stuff out of which all things are composed; the subject is dead, I can never say "I" again; there is no reality, only representations. These characterizations are variously imputed to postmodernism or poststructuralism, which are conflated with each other and sometimes conflated with deconstruction, and sometimes understood as an indiscriminate assemblage of French feminism, deconstruction, Lacanian psychoanalysis, Foucauldian analysis, Rorty's conversationalism, and cultural studies. On this side of the Atlantic and in recent discourse, the terms "postmodernism" or "poststructuralism" settle the differences among those positions in a single stroke, providing a substantive, a noun, that includes those positions as so many of its modalities or permutations. It may come as a surprise to some purveyors of the Continental scene to learn that Lacanian psychoanalysis in France positions itself officially against poststructuralism, that Kristeva denounces postmodernism,[2] that Foucauldians rarely relate to Derrideans, that Cixous and Irigaray are fundamentally opposed, and that the only tenuous connection between French feminism and deconstruction exists between Cixous and Derrida, although a certain affinity in textual practices is to be found between Derrida and Irigaray. Biddy Martin is also right to point out that almost all of French feminism adheres to a notion of high modernism and the avant-garde, which throws some question on whether these theories or writings can be grouped simply under the category of postmodernism.

I propose that the question of postmodernism be read not merely as the question that postmodernism poses for feminism, but as the question, what is postmodernism? What kind of existence does it have? Jean-François Lyotard champions the term, but he cannot be made into the example of what all the rest of the purported postmodernists are doing.[3] Lyotard's work is, for instance, seriously at odds with that of Derrida, who does not affirm the notion of "the postmodern," and with others for whom Lyotard is made to stand. Is he paradigmatic? Do all these theories have the same structure (a comforting notion to the critic who would dispense with them all at once)? Is the effort to colonize and domesticate these theories under the sign of the same, to group them synthetically and masterfully under a single rubric, a simple refusal to grant the specificity of these positions, an excuse not to read, and not to read closely? For if Lyotard uses the term, and if he can be conveniently grouped with a set of writers, and if some problematic quotation can be found in his work, then can that quotation serve as an "example" of postmodernism, symptomatic of the whole?

But if I understand part of the project of postmodernism, it is to call into question the ways in which such "examples" and "paradigms" serve to subordinate and erase that which they seek to explain. For the "whole," the field of postmodernism in its supposed breadth, is effectively "produced" by the example which is made to stand as a symptom and exemplar of the whole; in effect, if in the example of Lyotard we think we have a representation of postmodernism, we have then forced a substitution of the example for the entire field, effecting a violent reduction of the field to the one piece of text the critic is willing to read, a piece which, conveniently, uses the term "postmodern."

In a sense, this gesture of conceptual mastery that groups together a set of positions under the postmodern, that makes the postmodern into an epoch or a synthetic whole, and that claims that the part can stand for this artificially constructed whole, enacts a certain self-congratulatory ruse of power. It is paradoxical, at best, that the act of conceptual mastery that effects this dismissive grouping of positions under the postmodern wants to ward off the peril of political authoritarianism. For the assumption is that some piece of the text is representational, that it stands for the phenomenon, and that the structure of "these" positions can be properly and economically discerned in the structure of the one. What authorizes such an assumption from the start? From the start we must believe that theories offer themselves in bundles or in organized totalities, and that historically a set of theories which are structurally similar emerge as the articulation of an historically specific condition of human reflection. This Hegelian trope, which continues through Adorno, assumes from the start that these theories can be substituted for one another because they variously symptomatize a common structural preoccupation. And yet, that presumption can no longer be made, for the Hegelian presumption that a synthesis is available from the start is precisely what has come under contest in various ways by some of the positions happily unified under the sign of postmodernism. One might argue that if, and to the extent that, the postmodern functions as such a unifying sign, then it is a decidedly "modern" sign, which is why there is some question whether one can debate for or against this postmodernism. To install the term as that which can be only affirmed or negated is to force it to occupy one position within a binary, and so to affirm a logic of noncontradiction over and against some more generative scheme.

Perhaps the reason for this unification of positions is occasioned by the very unruliness of the field, by the way in which the differences among these positions cannot be rendered symptomatic, exemplary, or representative of each other and of some common structure called postmodernism. If postmodernism as a term has some force or meaning within social theory, or feminist social theory in particular, perhaps it can be found in the critical exercise that seeks to show how theory, how philosophy, is always implicated in power, and perhaps that is precisely what is symptomatically at work in the effort to domesticate and refuse a set of powerful criticisms under the rubric of postmodernism. That the philosophical apparatus in its various conceptual refinements is always engaged in exercising power is not a new insight, but then again the postmodern ought not to be confused with the new; after all, the pursuit of the "new" is the preoccupation of high modernism; if anything, the postmodern casts doubt upon the possibility of a "new" that is not in some way already implicated in the "old."

But the point articulated forcefully by some recent critics of normative political philosophy is that the recourse to a position—hypothetical, counterfactual, or imaginary—that places itself beyond the play of power, and which seeks to establish the metapolitical basis for a negotiation of power relations, is perhaps the most insidious ruse of power. That this position beyond power lays claim to its legitimacy through recourse to a prior and implicitly universal agreement does not in any way circumvent the charge, for what rationalist project will designate in advance what counts as agreement? What form of insidious cultural imperialism here legislates itself under the sign of the universal?[4]

I don't know about the term "postmodern," but if there is a point, and a fine point, to what I perhaps better understand as poststructuralism, it is that power pervades the very conceptual apparatus that seeks to negotiate its terms, including the subject position of the critic; and further, that this implication of the terms of criticism in the field of power is *not* the advent of a nihilistic relativism incapable of furnishing norms, but, rather, the very precondition of a politically engaged critique. To establish a set of norms that are beyond power or force is itself a powerful and forceful conceptual practice that sublimates, disguises, and extends its own power play through recourse to tropes of normative universality. And the point is not to do away with foundations, or even to champion a position that goes under the name of antifoundationalism. Both of those positions belong together as different versions of foundationalism and the skeptical problematic it engenders. Rather, the task is to interrogate what the theoretical move that establishes foundations *authorizes*, and what precisely it excludes or forecloses.

It seems that theory posits foundations incessantly, and forms implicit metaphysical commitments as a matter of course, even when it seeks to guard against it; foundations function as the unquestioned and the unquestionable within any theory. And yet, are these "foundations," that is, those premises that function as authorizing grounds, are they themselves not constituted through exclusions which, taken into account, expose the foundational premise as a contingent and contestable presumption? Even when we claim that there is some implied universal basis for a given foundation, that implication and that universality simply constitute a new dimension of unquestionability.

How is it that we might ground a theory or politics in a speech situation or subject position which is "universal," when the very category of the universal has only begun to be exposed for its own highly ethnocentric biases? How many "universalities" are there[5] and to what extent is cultural conflict understandable as the clashing of a set of presumed and intransigent "universalities," a conflict which cannot be negotiated through recourse to a culturally imperialist notion of the "universal" or, rather, which will only be solved through such recourse at the cost of violence? We have, I think, witnessed the conceptual and material violence of this practice in the United States's war against Iraq, in which the Arab "other" is understood to be radically "outside" the universal structures of reason and democracy and, hence, calls to be brought forcibly within. Significantly, the US had to abrogate the democratic principle of political sovereignty and free speech, among others, to effect this forcible return of Iraq to the "democratic" fold, and this violent move reveals, among other things, that such notions of universality are installed through the abrogation of the very universal principles to be implemented. Within the political context of contemporary postcoloniality more generally, it is perhaps especially urgent to underscore the very category of the "universal" as a site of insistent contest and resignification.[6] Given the contested character of the term, to assume from the start a procedural or substantive notion of the universal is of necessity to impose a culturally hegemonic notion on the social field. To herald that notion then as the philosophical instrument that will negotiate between conflicts of power is precisely to safeguard and reproduce a position of hegemonic power by installing it in the metapolitical site of ultimate normativity.

It may at first seem that I am simply calling for a more concrete and internally diverse "universality," a more synthetic and inclusive notion of universal, and in that way committed to the very foundational notion that I seek to undermine. But my task is, I think, significantly different from that which would articulate a comprehensive universality. In the first place, such a totalizing notion could only be achieved at the cost of producing new and further exclusions. The term "universality" would have to be left permanently open, permanently contested, permanently contingent, in order not to foreclose in advance future claims for inclusion. Indeed, from my position and from any historically constrained perspective, any totalizing concept of the universal will shut down rather than authorize the unanticipated and unanticipatable claims that will be made under the sign of "the universal." In this sense, I am not doing away with the category, but trying to relieve the category of its foundationalist weight in order to render it as a site of permanent political contest.

A social theory committed to democratic contestation within a postcolonial horizon needs to find a way to bring into question the foundations it is compelled to lay down. It is this movement of interrogating that ruse of authority that seeks to close itself off from contest that is, in my view, at the heart of any radical political project. Inasmuch as poststructuralism offers a mode of critique that effects this contestation of the foundationalist move, it can be used as a part of such a radical agenda. Note that I have said, "It can be used": I think there are no necessary political consequences for such a theory, but only a possible political deployment.

If one of the points associated with postmodernism is that the epistemological point of departure in philosophy is inadequate, then it ought not to be a question of subjects who claim to know and theorize under the sign of the postmodern pitted against other subjects who claim to know and theorize under the sign of the modern. Indeed, it is that very way of framing debate that is being contested by the suggestion that the position articulated by the subject is always in some way constituted by what must be displaced for that position to take hold, and that the subject who theorizes is constituted as a "theorizing subject" by a set of exclusionary and selective procedures. For, indeed, who is it that gets constituted as the feminist theorist whose framing of the debate will get publicity? Is it not always the case that power operates in advance, in the very procedures that establish who will be the subject who speaks in the name of feminism, and to whom? And is it not also clear that a process of subjection is presupposed in the subjectivating process that produces before you one speaking subject of feminist debate? What speaks when "I" speak to you? What are the institutional histories of subjection and subjectivation that "position" me here now? If there is something called "Butler's position," is this one that I devise, publish, and defend, that belongs to me as a kind of academic property? Or is there a grammar of the subject that merely encourages us to position me as the proprietor of those theories?

Indeed, how is it that a position becomes a position, for clearly not every utterance qualifies as such? It is clearly a matter of a certain authorizing power, and that clearly does not emanate from the position itself. My position is mine to the extent that "I"—and I do not shirk from the pronoun—replay and resignify the theoretical positions that have constituted me, working the possibilities of their convergence, and trying to take account of the possibilities that they systematically exclude. But it is clearly not the case that "I" preside over the positions that have constituted me, shuffling through them instrumentally, casting some aside, incorporating others, although some of my activity may take that form. The "I" who would select between them is always already constituted by them. The "I" is the transfer point of that replay, but it is simply not a strong enough claim to say that the "I" is situated; the "I," this "I," is *constituted* by these positions, and these "positions" are not merely theoretical products, but fully embedded organizing principles of material practices and institutional arrangements, those matrices of power and discourse that produce me as a viable "subject." Indeed, this "I" would not be a thinking, speaking "I" if it were not for the very positions that I oppose, for those positions, the ones that claim that the subject must be given in advance, that discourse is an instrument of reflection of that subject, are already part of what constitutes me.

No subject is its own point of departure; and the fantasy that it is one can only disavow its constitutive relations by recasting them as the domain of a countervailing externality. Indeed, one might consider Luce Irigaray's claim that the subject, understood as a fantasy of autogenesis, is always already masculine. Psychoanalytically, that version of the subject is constituted through a kind of disavowal or through the primary repression of its dependency on the maternal. And to become a *subject* on this model is surely not a feminist goal.

The critique of the subject is not a negation or repudiation of the subject, but, rather, a way of interrogating its construction as a pregiven or foundationalist premise. At the outset of the war against Iraq, we almost all saw strategists who placed before us maps of the Middle East, objects of analysis and targets of instrumental military action. Retired and active generals were called up by the networks to stand in for the generals on the field whose intentions would be invariably realized in the destruction of various Iraqi military bases. The various affirmations of the early success of these operations were delivered with great enthusiasm, and it seemed that this hitting of the goal, this apparently seamless realization of intention through an instrumental action without much resistance or hindrance was the occasion, not merely to destroy Iraqi military installations, but also to champion a masculinized Western subject whose will immediately translates into a deed, whose utterance or order materializes in an action which would destroy the very possibility of a reverse-strike, and whose obliterating power at once confirms the impenetrable contours of its own subjecthood.

It is perhaps interesting to remember at this juncture that Foucault linked the displacement of the intentional subject with modern power relations that he himself associated with war.[7] What he meant, I think, is that subjects who institute actions are themselves instituted effects of prior actions, and that the horizon in which we act is there as a constitutive possibility of our very capacity to act, not merely or exclusively as an exterior field or theater of operations. But perhaps more significantly, the actions instituted via that subject are part of a chain of actions that can no longer be understood as unilinear in direction or predictable in their outcomes. And yet, the instrumental military subject appears at first to utter words that materialize directly into destructive deeds. And throughout the war, it was as if the masculine Western subject preempted the divine power to translate words into deeds; the newscasters were almost all full of giddy happiness as they demonstrated, watched, vicariously enacted, the exactitude of destructiveness. As the war began, the words one would hear on television were "euphoria," and one newscaster remarked that US weapons were instruments of "terrible beauty" (CBS) and celebrated prematurely and phantasmatically their capacity to act instrumentally in the world to obliterate its opposition and to control the consequences of that obliteration. But the consequentiality of this act cannot be foreseen by the instrumental actor who currently celebrates the effectivity of its own intentions. What Foucault suggested was that this subject is itself the effect of a genealogy which is erased at the moment that the subject takes itself as the single origin of its action, and that the effects of an action always supersede the stated intention or purpose of the act. Indeed, the effects of the instrumental action always have the power to proliferate beyond the subject's control, indeed, to challenge the rational transparency of that subject's intentionality, and so to subvert the very definition of the subject itself. I suggest that we have been in the midst of a celebration on the part of the United States government and some of its allies of the phantasmatic subject, the one who determines its world unilaterally, and which is in some measure typified by the looming heads of retired generals framed against the map of the Middle East, where the speaking head of this subject is shown to be the same size, or larger, than the area it seeks to dominate. This is, in a sense, the graphics of the imperialist subject, a visual allegory of the action itself.

But here you think that I have made a distinction between the action itself and something like a representation, but I want to make a stronger point. You will perhaps have noticed that Colin Powell, the chairman of the Joint Chiefs of Staff, invoked what is, I think, a new military convention of calling the sending of missiles "the delivery of an ordnance." The phrase is significant, I think; it figures an act of violence as an act of law (the military term "ordnance" is linked etymologically to the juridical "ordinance"), and so wraps the destruction in the appearance of orderliness; but in addition, it figures the missile as a kind of command, an order to obey, and is thus itself figured as a certain act of speech which not only delivers a message—get out of Kuwait—but effectively enforces that message through the threat of death and through death itself. Of course, this is a message that can never be received, for it kills its addressee, and so it is not an ordinance at all, but the failure of all ordinances, the refusal of a communication. And for those who remain to read the message, they will not read what is sometimes quite literally written on the missile.

Throughout the war, we witnessed and participated in the conflation of the television screen and the lens of the bomber pilot. In this sense, the visual record of this war is not a *reflection* on the war, but the enactment of its phantasmatic structure, indeed, part of the very means by which it is socially constituted and maintained as a war. The so-called "smart bomb" records its target as it moves in to destroy it—a bomb with a camera attached in front, a kind of optical phallus; it relays that film back to a command control and that film is refilmed on television, effectively constituting the television screen and its viewer as the extended apparatus of the bomb itself. In this sense, by viewing we are bombing, identified with both bomber and bomb, flying through space, transported from the North American continent to Iraq, and yet securely wedged in the couch in our own living room. The smart-bomb screen is, of course, destroyed in the moment that it enacts its destruction, which is to say that this is a recording of a thoroughly destructive act which can never record that destructiveness, indeed, which effects the phantasmatic distinction between the hit and its consequences. Thus as viewers, we veritably enact the allegory of military triumph: we retain our visual distance and our bodily safety through the disembodied enactment of the kill that produces no blood and in which we retain our radical impermeability. In this sense, we are in relation to this site of destruction absolutely proximate, absolutely essential, and absolutely distant, a figure for imperial power which takes the aerial, global view, the disembodied killer who can never be killed, the sniper as a figure for imperialist military power. The television screen thus redoubles the aerial view, securing a fantasy of transcendence, of a disembodied instrument of destruction which is infinitely protected from a reverse-strike through the guarantee of electronic distance.

This aerial view never comes close to seeing the *effects* of its destruction, and as a close-up to the site becomes increasingly possible, the screen conveniently destroys itself. And so although it was made to seem that this was a humane bombing, one which took buildings and military installations as its targets, this was, on the contrary, the effect of a frame which excluded from view the systemic destruction of a population, what Foucault calls the modern dream of states.[8] Or perhaps we ought to state it otherwise: precisely through excluding its targets from view under the rubric of proving the capacity to target precisely, this is a frame that effectively performs the annihilation that it systematically derealizes.

The demigod of a U.S. military subject which euphorically enacted the fantasy that it can achieve its aims with ease fails to understand that its actions have produced effects that will far exceed its phantasmatic purview; it thinks that its goals were achieved in a matter of weeks, and that its action was completed. But the action continues to act after the intentional subject has announced its completion. The effects of its actions have already inaugurated violence in places and in ways that it not only could not foresee but will be unable ultimately to contain, effects which will produce a massive and violent contestation of the Western subject's phantasmatic self-construction.

If I can, then, I'll try to return to the subject at hand. In a sense, the subject is constituted through an exclusion and differentiation, perhaps a repression, that is subsequently concealed, covered over, by

the effect of autonomy. In this sense, autonomy is the logical consequence of a disavowed dependency, which is to say that the autonomous subject can maintain the illusion of its autonomy insofar as it
covers over the break out of which it is constituted. This dependency
and this break are already social relations, ones which precede and
condition the formation of the subject. As a result, this is not a relation in which the subject finds itself, as one of the relations that
forms its situation. The subject is constructed through acts of differentiation that distinguish the subject from its constitutive outside, a
domain of abjected alterity conventionally associated with the feminine, but clearly not exclusively. Precisely in this recent war we saw
"the Arab" figured as the abjected other as well as a site of homo-
phobic fantasy made clear in the abundance of bad jokes grounded in
the linguistic sliding from Saddam to Sodom.

There is no ontologically intact reflexivity to the subject which is
then placed within a cultural context; that cultural context, as it
were, is already there as the disarticulated process of that subject's
production, one that is concealed by the frame that would situate a
ready-made subject in an external web of cultural relations.

We may be tempted to think that to assume the subject in advance
is necessary in order to safeguard the *agency* of the subject. But to
claim that the subject is constituted is not to claim that it is determined; on the contrary, the constituted character of the subject is the
very precondition of its agency. For what is it that enables a purpo-
sive and significant reconfiguration of cultural and political relations,
if not a relation that can be turned against itself, reworked, resisted?
Do we need to assume theoretically from the start a subject with
agency *before* we can articulate the terms of a significant social and
political task of transformation, resistance, radical democratization?
If we do not offer in advance the theoretical guarantee of that agent,
are we doomed to give up transformation and meaningful political
practice? My suggestion is that agency belongs to a way of thinking
about persons as instrumental actors who confront an external political field. But if we agree that politics and power exist already at the
level at which the subject and its agency are articulated and made
possible, then agency can be *presumed* only at the cost of refusing to
inquire into its construction. Consider that "agency" has no formal
existence or, if it does, it has no bearing on the question at hand. In a
sense, the epistemological model that offers us a pregiven subject or
agent is one that refuses to acknowledge that *agency is always and*

only a political prerogative. As such, it seems crucial to question the conditions of its possibility, not to take it for granted as an a priori guarantee. We need instead to ask, what possibilities of mobilization are produced on the basis of existing configurations of discourse and power? Where are the possibilities of reworking that very matrix of power by which we are constituted, of reconstituting the legacy of that constitution, and of working against each other those processes of regulation that can destabilize existing power regimes? For if the subject is constituted by power, that power does not cease at the moment the subject is constituted, for that subject is never fully constituted, but is subjected and produced time and again. That subject is neither a ground nor a product, but the permanent possibility of a certain resignifying process, one which gets detoured and stalled through other mechanisms of power, but which is power's own possibility of being reworked. It is not enough to say that the subject is invariably engaged in a political field; that phenomenological phrasing misses the point that the subject is an accomplishment regulated and produced in advance. And is as such fully political; indeed, perhaps *most* political at the point in which it is claimed to be prior to politics itself. To perform this kind of Foucauldian critique of the subject is not to do away with the subject or pronounce its death, but merely to claim that certain versions of the subject are politically insidious.

For the subject to be a pregiven point of departure for politics is to defer the question of the political construction and regulation of the subject itself; for it is important to remember that subjects are constituted through exclusion, that is, through the creation of a domain of deauthorized subjects, presubjects, figures of abjection, populations erased from view. This becomes clear, for instance, within the law when certain qualifications must first be met in order to be, quite literally, a claimant in sex discrimination or rape cases. Here it becomes quite urgent to ask who qualifies as a "who," what systematic structures of disempowerment make it impossible for certain injured parties to invoke the "I" effectively within a court of law? Or less overtly, in a social theory like Albert Memmi's *The Colonizer and the Colonized*, an otherwise compelling call for radical enfranchisement, the category of women falls into neither category, the oppressor or the oppressed.[9] How do we theorize the exclusion of women from the category of the oppressed? Here the construction of subject-positions works to exclude women from the description of oppression, and this constitutes a different kind of oppression, one that is effected by the very *erasure* that grounds the articulation of the emancipatory subject. As Joan Scott makes clear in *Gender and the Politics of History*, once it is understood that subjects are formed through exclusionary operations, it becomes politically necessary to trace the operations of that construction and erasure.[10]

The above sketches in part a Foucauldian reinscription of the subject, an effort to resignify the subject as a site of resignification. As a result, it is not a "bidding farewell" to the subject per se, but, rather, a call to rework that notion outside the terms of an epistemological given. But perhaps Foucault is not really postmodern; after all, his is an analytics of *modern* power. There is, of course, talk about the death of the subject, but *which* subject is that? And what is the status of the utterance that announces its passing? What speaks now that the subject is dead? That there is a speaking seems clear, for how else could the utterance be heard? So clearly, the death of that subject is not the end of agency, of speech, or of political debate. There is the refrain that, just now, when women are beginning to assume the place of subjects, postmodern positions come along to announce that the subject is dead (there is a difference between positions of poststructuralism which claim that the subject *never* existed, and postmodern positions which claim that the subject *once* had integrity, but no longer does). Some see this as a conspiracy against women and other disenfranchised groups who are now only beginning to speak on their own behalf. But what precisely is meant by this, and how do we account for the very strong criticisms of the subject as an instrument of Western imperialist hegemony theorized by Gloria Anzaldua,[11] Gayatri Spivak[12] and various theorists of postcoloniality? Surely there is a caution offered here, that in the very struggle toward enfranchisement and democratization, we might adopt the very models of domination by which we were oppressed, not realizing that one way that domination works is through the regulation and production of subjects. Through what exclusions has the feminist subject been constructed, and how do those excluded domains return to haunt the "integrity" and "unity" of the feminist "we"? And how is it that the very category, the subject, the "we," that is supposed to be presumed for the purpose of solidarity, produces the very factionalization it is supposed to quell? Do women want to become subjects on the model which requires and produces an anterior region of abjection, or must feminism become a process which is self-critical about the processes that produce and destabilize identity categories? To take the construction of the subject as a political problematic is not the same as doing away with the subject; to deconstruct the subject is not to negate or throw away the concept; on the contrary, deconstruction implies only that we suspend all commitments to that to which the term, "the subject," refers, and that we consider the linguistic functions it serves in the consolidation and concealment of authority. To deconstruct is not to negate or to dismiss, but to call into question and, perhaps most importantly, to open up a term, like the subject, to a reusage or redeployment that previously has not been authorized.

Within feminism, it seems as if there is some political necessity to speak as and for *women*, and I would not contest that necessity. Surely, that is the way in which representational politics operates, and in this country, lobbying efforts are virtually impossible without recourse to identity politics. So we agree that demonstrations and legislative efforts and radical movements need to make claims in the name of women.

But this necessity needs to be reconciled with another. The minute that the category of women is invoked as *describing* the constituency for which feminism speaks, an internal debate invariably begins over what the descriptive content of that term will be. There are those who claim that there is an ontological specificity to women as childbearers that forms the basis of a specific legal and political interest in representation, and then there are others who understand maternity to be a social relation that is, under current social circumstances, the specific and cross-cultural situation of women. And there are those who seek recourse to Gilligan and others to establish a feminine specificity that makes itself clear in women's communities or ways of knowing. But every time that specificity is articulated, there is resistance and factionalization within the very constituency that is supposed to be *unified* by the articulation of its common element. In the 1980s, the feminist "we" rightly came under attack by women of color who claimed that the "we" was invariably white, and that that "we" that was meant to solidify the movement was the very source of a painful factionalization. The effort to characterize a feminine specificity through recourse to maternity, whether biological or social, produced a similar factionalization and even a disavowal of feminism altogether. For surely all women are not mothers; some cannot be, some are too young or too old to be, some choose not to be, and for some who are mothers, that is not necessarily the rallying point of their politicization in feminism.

I would argue that any effort to give universal or specific content to the category of women, presuming that that guarantee of solidarity is required *in advance*, will necessarily produce factionalization, and that "identity" as a point of departure can never hold as the solidifying ground of a feminist political movement. Identity categories are never merely descriptive, but always normative, and as such, exclusionary. This is not to say that the term "women" ought not to be used, or that we ought to announce the death of the category. On the contrary, if feminism presupposes that "women" designates an undesignatable field of differences, one that cannot be totalized or summarized by a descriptive identity category, then the very term becomes a site of permanent openness and resignifiability. I would argue that the rifts among women over the content of the term ought to be safeguarded and prized, indeed, that this constant rifting ought to be affirmed as the ungrounded ground of feminist theory. To deconstruct the subject of feminism is not, then, to censure its usage, but, on the contrary, to release the term into a future of multiple significations, to emancipate it from the maternal or racialist ontologies to which it has been restricted, and to give it play as a site where unanticipated meanings might come to bear.

Paradoxically, it may be that only through releasing the category of women from a fixed referent that something like "agency" becomes possible. For if the term permits of a resignification, if its referent is not fixed, then possibilities for new configurations of the term become possible. In a sense, what women signify has been taken for granted for too long, and what has been fixed as the "referent" of the term has been "fixed," normalized, immobilized, paralyzed in positions of subordination. In effect, the signified has been conflated with the referent, whereby a set of meanings have been taken to inhere in the real nature of women themselves. To recast the referent as the signified, and to authorize or safeguard the category of women as a site of possible resignifications is to expand the possibilities of what it means to be a woman and in this sense to condition and enable an enhanced sense of agency.

One might well ask: but doesn't there have to be a set of norms that discriminate between those descriptions that ought to adhere to the category of women and those that do not? The only answer to that question is a counter-question: who would set those norms, and what contestations would they produce? To establish a normative foundation for settling the question of what ought properly to be included in the description of women would be only and always to produce a new site of political contest. That foundation would settle nothing, but would of its own necessity founder on its own authoritarian ruse. This is not to say that there is no foundation, but rather, that wherever there is one, there will also be a foundering, a contestation. That such foundations exist only to be put into question is, as it were, the permanent risk of the process of democratization. To refuse that contest is to sacrifice the radical democratic impetus of feminist politics. That the category is unconstrained, even that it comes to serve antifeminist purposes, will be part of the risk of this procedure. But this is a risk that is produced by the very foundationalism that seeks to safeguard feminism against it. In a sense, this risk is the foundation, and hence is not, of any feminist practice.

In the final part of this paper, I would like to turn to a related question, one that emerges from the concern that a feminist theory cannot proceed without presuming the materiality of women's bodies, the materiality of sex. The chant of antipostmodernism runs, if everything is discourse, then is there no reality to bodies? How do we understand the material violence that women suffer? In responding to this criticism, I would like to suggest that the very formulation misconstrues the critical point.

I don't know what postmodernism is, but I do have some sense of what it might mean to subject notions of the body and materiality to a deconstructive critique. To deconstruct the concept of matter or that of bodies is not to negate or refuse either term. To deconstruct these terms means, rather, to continue to use them, to repeat them, to repeat them subversively, and to displace them from the contexts in which they have been deployed as instruments of oppressive power. Here it is of course necessary to state quite plainly that the options for theory are not exhausted by *presuming* materiality, on the one hand, and *negating* materiality, on the other. It is my purpose to do precisely neither of these. To call a presupposition into question is not the same as doing away with it: rather, it is to free it up from its metaphysical lodgings in order to occupy and to serve very different political aims. To problematize the matter of bodies entails in the first instance a loss of epistemological certainty, but this loss of certainty does not necessarily entail political nihilism as its result.[13]

If a deconstruction of the materiality of bodies suspends and problematizes the traditional ontological referent of the term, it does not freeze, banish, render useless, or deplete of meaning the usage of the term; on the contrary, it provides the conditions to *mobilize* the signifier in the service of an alternative production.

Consider that most material of concepts, "sex," which Monique Wittig calls a thoroughly political category, and which Michel Foucault calls a regulatory and "fictitious unity." For both theorists, sex does not *describe* a prior materiality, but produces and regulates the *intelligibility* of the *materiality* of bodies. For both, and in different ways, the category of sex imposes a duality and a uniformity on bodies in order to maintain reproductive sexuality as a compulsory order. I've argued elsewhere more precisely how this works, but for our purposes, I would like to suggest that this kind of categorization can be called a violent one, a forceful one, and that this discursive ordering and production of bodies in accord with the category of sex is itself a material violence.

The violence of the letter, the violence of the mark which establishes what will and will not signify, what will and will not be included within the intelligible, takes on a political significance when the letter is the law or the authoritative legislation of what will be the materiality of sex.

So what can this kind of poststructural analysis tell us about violence and suffering? Is it perhaps that forms of violence are to be understood as more pervasive, more constitutive, and more insidious than prior models have allowed us to see? That is part of the point of the previous discussion of war, but let me now make it differently in yet another context.

Consider the legal restrictions that regulate what does and does not count as rape: here the politics of violence operate through regulating what will and will not be able to appear as an effect of violence.[14] There is, then, already in this foreclosure a violence at work, a marking off in advance of what will or will not qualify under the signs of "rape" or "government violence," or in the case of states in which twelve separate pieces of empirical evidence are required to establish "rape," what can then be called a governmentally facilitated rape.

A similar line of reasoning is at work in discourses on rape when the "sex" of a woman is claimed as that which establishes the responsibility for her own violation. The defense attorney in the New Bedford gang-rape case asked the plaintiff, "If you're living with a man, what are you doing running around the streets getting raped?"[15] The "running around" in this sentence collides grammatically with "getting raped": "getting" is procuring, acquiring, having, as if this were a treasure she was running around after, but "getting raped" suggests the passive voice. Literally, of course, it would be difficult to be "running around" and be "getting raped" at the same time, which suggests that there must be an elided passage here, perhaps a directional that leads from the former to the latter? If the sense of the sentence is, "running around [looking to get] raped," which seems to be the only logical way of bridging the two parts of the sentence, then rape as a passive acquisition is precisely the object of her active search. The first clause suggests that she "belongs" at home, with her man, that the home is a site in which she is the domestic property of that man, and the "streets" establish her as open season. If she is looking to get raped, she is looking to become the property of some other, and this objective is installed in her desire, conceived here as quite frantic in its pursuit. She is "running around," suggesting that she is running around looking under every rock for a rapist to satisfy her. Significantly, the phrase installs as the structuring principle of her desire "getting raped," where "rape" is figured as an act of willful self-expropriation. Since becoming the property of a man is the objective of her "sex," articulated in and through her sexual desire, and rape is the way in which that appropriation occurs "on the street" [a logic that implies that rape is to marriage as the streets are to the home, that is, that "rape" is street marriage, a marriage without a home, a marriage for homeless girls, and that marriage is domesticated rape], then "rape" is the logical consequence of the enactment of her sex and sexuality outside domesticity. Never mind that this rape took place in a bar, for the "bar" is, within this imaginary, but an extension of the "street," or perhaps its exemplary moment, for there is no enclosure, that is, no protection, other than the *home* as domestic marital space. In any case, the single cause of her violation is here figured as her "sex" which, given its natural propensity to seek expropriation, once dislocated from domestic propriety, naturally pursues its rape and is thus responsible for it.

The category of sex here functions as a principle of production and regulation at once, the cause of the violation installed as the formative principle of the body is sexuality. Here sex is a category, but not merely a representation; it is a principle of production, intelligibility, and regulation which enforces a violence and rationalizes it after the fact. The very terms by which the violation is explained *enact* the violation, and concede that the violation was under way before it takes the empirical form of a criminal act. That rhetorical enactment *shows* that "violence" is produced through the foreclosure effected by this analysis, through the erasure and negation that determines the field of appearances and intelligibility of crimes of culpability. As a category that effectively produces the political meaning of what it describes, "sex" here works its silent "violence" in regulating what is and is not designatable.

I place the terms "violence" and "sex" under quotation marks: is this the sign of a certain deconstruction, the end to politics? Or am I underscoring the iterable structure of these terms, the ways in which they yield to a repetition, occur ambiguously, and am I doing that precisely to further a political analysis? I place them in quotation marks to show that they are under contest, up for grabs, to initiate the contest, to question their traditional deployment, and call for some other. The quotation marks do not place into question the urgency or credibility of sex or violence as political issues, but, rather, show that the way their very materiality is circumscribed is fully political. The effect of the quotation marks is to denaturalize the terms, to designate these signs as sites of political debate.

If there is a fear that, by no longer being able to take for granted the subject, its gender, its sex, or its materiality, feminism will founder, it might be wise to consider the political consequences of keeping in their place the very premises that have tried to secure our subordination from the start.

Notes

This paper was first presented in a different version as "Feminism and the Question of Postmodernism" at the Greater Philadelphia Philosophy Consortium in September 1990.

1. Here it is worth noting that in some recent political theory, notably in the writings of Ernesto Laclau and Chantal Mouffe (*Hegemony and Socialist Strategy*, London: Verso, 1986), William Connolly (*Political Theory and Modernity*, Madison: University of Wisconsin Press, 1988), as well as Jean-Luc Nancy and Philippe Lacoue-Labarthe ("Le retrait du politique" in *Le Retrait du politique*, Paris: Editions Galilée, 1983), there is an insistence that the political field is of necessity constructed through the production of a determining exterior. In other words, the very domain of politics constitutes itself through the production and naturalization of the "pre-" or "non-" political. In Derridean terms, this is the production of a "constitutive outside." Here I would like to suggest a distinction between the constitution of a political field that produces *and naturalizes* that constitutive outside and a political field that produces and *renders contingent* the specific parameters of that constitutive outside. Although I do not think that the differential relations through which the political field itself is constituted can ever be fully elaborated (precisely because the status of that elaboration would have to be elaborated as well *ad infinitum*), I do find useful William Connolly's notion of constitutive antagonisms, a notion that finds a parallel expression in Laclau and Mouffe, which suggests a form of political struggle which puts the parameters of the political itself into question. This is especially important for feminist concerns insofar as the grounds of politics ("universality," "equality," "the subject of rights" have been constructed through unmarked racial and gender exclusions and by a conflation of politics with public life that renders the private (reproduction, domains of "femininity") prepolitical.

2. Julia Kristeva, *Black Sun: Depression and Melancholy* (New York: Columbia University Press, 1989), pp. 258–259.

3. The conflation of Lyotard with the array of thinkers summarily positioned under the rubric of "postmodernism" is performed by the title and essay by Seyla Benhabib: "Epistemologies of Postmodernism: A Rejoinder to Jean-François Lyotard," in *Feminism/Postmodernism*, edited by Linda Nicholson (New York: Routledge, 1989).

4. This is abundantly clear in feminist criticisms of Jürgen Habermas as well as Catharine MacKinnon. See Iris Young, "Impartiality and the Civic Public: Some Implications of Feminist Criticisms of Modern Political Theory," in Seyla Benhabib and Drucilla Cornell, eds., *Feminism as Critique: Essays on the Politics of Gender in Late-Capitalism*, (Oxford: Basil Blackwell, 1987); Nancy Fraser, *Unruly Practices: Power and Gender in Contemporary Social Theory* Minneapolis: University of Minnesota Press, 1989; especially "What's Critical about Critical Theory: The Case of Habermas and Gender", Wendy Brown, "Razing Consciousness", *The Nation*, 250:2, January 8–15, 1990.

5. See Ashis Nandy on the notion of alternative universalities in the preface to *The Intimate Enemy: Loss and Recovery of Self under Colonialism*, (New Delhi: Oxford University Press, 1983).

6. Homi Bhabha's notion of "hybridity" is important to consider in this context. See *The Location of Culture* (New York: Routledge, 1994).

7. Michel Foucault, *The History of Sexuality, Vol. I: An Introduction*, translated by Robert Hurley (New York: Random House, 1980), p. 102.

8. "Wars are no longer waged in the name of sovereign who must be defended: they are waged on behalf of the existence of everyone: entire populations are mobilized for the purpose of wholesale slaughter in the name of life necessity: massacres," he writes, "have become vital." He later adds, "the principle underlying the tactics of battle—that one has to be capable of killing in order to go on living—has become the principle that defines the strategy of states. But the existence in question is no longer the juridical existence of sovereignty: at stake is the biological existence of a population. If genocide is indeed the dream of modern powers, this is not because of a recent return of the ancient right to kill; it is because power is situated and exercised at the level of life, the species, the race, and the large-scale phenomena of population." Foucault, *The History of Sexuality*. p. 137.

9. "At the height of the revolt," Memmi writes, "the colonized still bears the traces and lessons of prolonged cohabitation (just as the smile or movements of a wife, even during divorce proceedings, remind one strangely of those of her husband)." Here Memmi sets up an analogy which presumes that colonizer and colonized exist in a parallel and separate relation to the divorcing husband and wife. The analogy simultaneously and paradoxically suggests the feminization of the colonized, where the colonized is presumed to be the subject of men, *and* the exclusion of the women from the category of the colonized subject. Albert Memmi, *The Colonizer and the Colonized*, (Boston: Beacon Press, 1965), p. 129.

10. Joan W. Scott, *Gender and the Politics of History*, (New York: Columbia University Press), 1988, introduction.

11. Gloria Anzaldua, *La Frontera/Borderlands*, (San Francisco: Spinsters Ink, 1988).

12. Gayatri Spivak, "Can the Subaltern Speak?" in *Marxism and the Interpretation of Culture*, eds. Nelson and Grossberg. (Chicago: University of Illinois Press, 1988).

13. The body posited as prior to the sign, is always *posited* or *signified as prior*. This signification works through producing an *effect* of its own procedure, the body that it nevertheless and simultaneously claims to discover as that which *precedes* signification. If the body signified as prior to signification is an effect of signification, then the mimetic or representational status of language, which claims that signs follow bodies as their necessary mirrors, is not mimetic at all; on the contrary, it is productive, constitutive, one might even argue *performative*, inasmuch as this signifying act produces the body that it then claims to find prior to any and all signification.

14. For an extended analysis of the relationship of language and rape, see Sharon Marcus in *Feminists Theorize the Political*, eds. Judith Butler and Joan W. Scott (New York: Routledge, 1992).

15. Quoted in Catharine MacKinnon, *Toward a Feminist Theory of the State*, (Boston: Harvard University Press, 1989), p. 171.

3

False Antitheses:
A Response to Seyla Benhabib
and Judith Butler

Nancy Fraser

Ostensibly, Seyla Benhabib's and Judith Butler's papers dispute the relationship of feminism to postmodernism.[1] However, in the course of their exchange, a debate about "modernity" versus "postmodernity" is transmuted into a debate over the relative merits of Critical Theory and poststructuralism. Benhabib defends a feminism rooted in Critical Theory and premised on concepts of autonomy, critique, and utopia. Butler's feminism, in contrast, rests on poststructuralist conceptions of subjectivity, identity, and human agency that are at odds with Benhabib's. Benhabib claims that postmodernist and poststructuralist views of subjectivity are incompatible with feminist politics, moreover, while Butler claims that views like Benhabib's imply an authoritarian foundationalism antithetical to the feminist project. Finally, to complicate matters still further, the two writers disagree about to how to characterize their disagreement. For Benhabib, the issue that divides them is whether postmodernist proclamations of "the death of man," "the death of history," and "the death of metaphysics" can support a feminist politics. For Butler, the question is whether postmodernism really exists except in the paranoid fantasies of those seeking secure foundations for feminist politics in unproblematized metaphysical notions.

Evidently, Benhabib and Butler disagree not only about postmodernism but also about the relative merits of Critical Theory and post-

59

structuralism. At first sight, their views seem irreconcilably opposed. Certainly, each believes her position excludes the other's. Thus, despite their manifold disagreements, there is one issue on which they agree. Both assume that the only way to resolve this dispute is to choose between Critical Theory and poststructuralism; there is no way that feminists can have both. But is that really the only possibility? The apparent necessity of opting for one approach and rejecting the other creates difficulties for readers, like me, who think each has something important to offer to feminists.

I contend that feminists do not have to choose between Critical Theory and poststructuralism; instead, we might reconstruct each approach so as to reconcile it with the other. Thus, in what follows, I shall argue that the Benhabib-Butler exchange poses false antitheses and unnecessary polarizations. To make this case I shall identify the respective strengths and weaknesses of each paper, subjecting to special scrutiny those formulations of each position that purport definitively to rule out the other. In particular I shall indicate points at which each theorist has overreached herself by extrapolating to the point of implausibility an insight that is otherwise sound. In those cases, I shall propose more modest and defensible alternative formulations that avoid generating a false antithesis between Critical Theory and poststructuralism. My overall aim is to preserve the best elements of each paradigm, thereby helping to prepare the ground for their fruitful integration in feminist theorizing.

Let me begin with Seyla Benhabib's paper, which evinces her usual clarity, comprehensiveness, and political commitment. Benhabib argues that feminists should not rush too quickly into an alliance with postmodernism despite certain apparent affinities. To be sure, postmodernists and feminists have both criticized traditional philosophical concepts of man, history, and metaphysics, but their criticisms do not necessarily converge. On the contrary, there are postmodernist versions of "the death of man," "the death of history," and "the death of metaphysics" that are not compatible with feminism. Thus, it is necessary to distinguish strong and weak versions of those theses. Feminists may, indeed should, accept the weak versions, but the strong versions must be decisively rejected.

According to Benhabib, a strong postmodernist version of "the death of man" undermines the principles of autonomy and self-reflective subjectivity on which feminist politics depends. Likewise, a strong postmodern interpretation of "the death of history" precludes the possibility of an emancipatory interest in the past, including the reconstruction of women's history. Finally, a strong version of "the death of metaphysics" undermines the possibility of radical feminist critique that goes beyond immanent criticism. Together these three strong postmodernist theses are tantamount to a disabling "retreat from utopia." Feminists should therefore reject them in favor of weaker, nondisabling versions of the death of man, the death of history, and the death of metaphysics.

Here Benhabib has elaborated a clarifying and fruitful argumentative strategy. By identifying these theses and distinguishing strong and weak versions of each, she suggests a way to overcome problems that typically plague debates about postmodernism. Too often, such debates swirl confusedly around sweeping statements that conflate analytically distinct claims. Benhabib's approach of sorting out weaker and stronger versions of such claims enables more nuanced and fruitful discussion.

However, Benhabib does not herself use this approach to fullest advantage. In each case, she targets a postmodernist thesis that is too strong and too easily refutable. Then, having "refuted postmodernism," she claims to have established her critical-theoretical alternative. The latter claim is not persuasive, however, since she has not considered other versions of the theses. She overlooks medium-strength versions that do not pose a false antithesis between Critical Theory and poststructuralism and are theoretically defensible and politically enabling.

Take, for example, her discussion of the death of history. This theme has been salient in poststructuralist criticisms of Marxism, some of which propose to throw out the baby of politically engaged historical reflection with the bathwater of teleology.[2] In the face of such overreactions, Benhabib quite sensibly wants a view that allows for engaged historiography while ruling out essentialist, monocausal metanarratives that enshrine a single group as the subject of history. The thrust of her argument is to define a middle ground between modernist metanarratives and strong postmodernisms that would liquidate history altogether. But just when the argument demands some characterization of that middle ground, and of the sort of historiography that might occupy it, Benhabib's reasoning wavers. Instead of staking out the middle position that her own argument requires, she concludes by doubting that feminist historiography can be postmodern in *any* sense and still retain an interest in emancipation.

En route to this conclusion, Benhabib responds ambivalently to one approach that *does* stake out the middle position: the version of post-modernist feminism elaborated by Linda Nicholson and me in our paper, "Social Criticism Without Philosophy: An Encounter between Feminism and Postmodernism."[3] There Nicholson and I opposed interpretations of the death of history that would preclude "big" histories of male dominance. We distinguished metanarratives, which claim to provide foundational grounding in a philosophy of history, from large-scale empirical narratives, which are fallibilistic and non-foundational. This distinction permits feminists to reject metanarrative but still affirm historiography that discerns broad patterns of gender relations over large stretches of time.[4] It thereby helps secure one of the intellectual tools we need to understand a phenomenon as large and complex as male dominance. Moreover, because our view allows both for large historical narrative and for smaller local narrative, it permits each to counteract the distorting tendencies of the other: local genealogizing narratives correct the tendency of large-scale accounts to congeal into "quasi-metanarratives," while larger contextualizing accounts help prevent local narratives from devolving into simple demonstrations of "difference." Nicholson and I concluded that the result would be a postmodernist, pragmatic, fallibilistic mode of feminist theorizing that would retain social-critical, emancipatory force even as it eschewed philosophical foundations. It would also be a mode of feminist theorizing that overcomes the false antithesis between Critical Theory and poststructuralism by integrating the best insights of each.

Benhabib endorses our defense of "big" historiography but rejects our model of postmodernist, pragmatic, fallibilistic feminist theorizing. She contends the latter precludes historiography guided by an emancipatory interest and permits only value-free social science. Unfortunately, she offers no argument in support of this contention. Does she mean to imply that only metanarrative can guarantee an emancipatory interest in history?[5] That view posits a false antithesis between antifoundationalism and political engagement. Not only is it at odds with Benhabib's stated position, but it is also belied by the many forms of engaged historiography now being practiced by feminist scholars without any recourse to metanarrative. These include local histories that recover lost traditions of female agency or resistance; narratives that restore historicity to female-centered practices heretofore misapprehended as natural; histories that revalue previously derogated forms of women's culture; and genealogies that denaturalize gender-coded categories like "production" and "reproduction" or that reconstruct the hidden gender subtexts of concepts like "class" and the "state."[6] *Pace* Benhabib, all these genres of feminist historiography can be characterized as postmodern insofar as they refuse to legitimate themselves by recourse to the philosophy of history. Yet all are clearly guided by an interest in women's liberation, and all have emancipatory effects. Moreover, even their refusal to ground themselves by appeal to a foundational metanarrative is motivated by an interest in emancipation, namely, the interest in avoiding the vanguardism associated with claims about the subject and telos of history.

For these reasons Nicholson's and my view still seems to me a theoretically defensible and politically enabling version of the death of history. It is a version, moreover, that fulfills Benhabib's stated aim of avoiding the untenable extremes. Why then does she shrink from accepting it? Perhaps she fears that unless we can anchor the feminist interest in emancipation in a metanarrative, that interest will be arbitrary and unjustified. If that is Benhabib's real worry, then the question of the death of history collapses into the question of the death of metaphysics.

Benhabib's treatment of the death of metaphysics evinces analogous problems. She rejects a strong version that would preclude warranted social critique altogether, but she does not wish to ground critique in a foundationalist epistemology. She is poised therefore to articulate a weak version of the death of metaphysics. However, in the course of her argument, she swerves from that goal and posits a series of false antitheses.

The steps in her argument are as follows. First, Benhabib endorses the view, shared by Rorty, Lyotard, Nicholson, and me, that there can be no justificatory metadiscourse that articulates the validity criteria for every first-order discourse. Next, she rejects the alternative of a naturalized epistemology that would merely describe existing practices of social criticism and surrender all normative claims. Somewhere between these extremes, she implies, is a third alternative, which would elaborate a view of *situated* social criticism and account for its possibility. Unfortunately, Benhabib does not develop this alternative. Instead of pursuing the logic of her argument, she concludes that situated criticism is not good enough and that therefore there can be no social criticism without philosophy.[7]

Why does Benhabib believe that situated social criticism is not good enough? She offers two arguments to support her view, but neither is ultimately persuasive. The first is that situated criticism presupposes an "unjustified hermeneutical monism of meaning." It supposes, in other words, that cultural practices have a single, consistent, univocal meaning, which the critic can read off straightforwardly and unproblematically. But this is belied by the fact that traditions are contested, interpretations conflict, and social practices do not wear their meanings on their sleeves. It follows, claims Benhabib, that social criticism cannot consist merely in elucidating cultural norms that are given in social practices and traditions. There is no avoiding the *philosophical* task of clarifying and reconstructing the norms to which criticism appeals. Thus, according to Benhabib, social criticism without philosophy is impossible.

But is it really? Everything depends on what is meant by the terms "situated criticism" and "philosophy." The position that Benhabib has criticized here is Michael Walzer's, and she is right to point out its shortcomings.[8] What she overlooks is that Walzer's is not the only available view of situated criticism. Other versions appreciate the essential contestedness of culture and the need to clarify and reconstruct cultural norms. But they hold that practices of clarifying and reconstructing norms are themselves culturally and historically situated and cannot escape that condition. Thus, on this view, both criticism and its self-clarification are situated. Neither requires philosophy, moreover, if "philosophy" means discourse aspiring to the God's-eye view of foundationalist thought. Indeed, the self-clarification of social criticism need not take the form of general conceptual reflection pursued in isolation from historical, legal, cultural, and sociological inquiry.[9] It may also take the form of contextualizing historical narrative that genealogizes norms and thereby situates them more precisely.[10] Finally, it is worth noting that situated criticism does not preclude general claims or appeals to general norms; it only requires that these, too, be regarded as situated. Thus, for a variety of reasons, Benhabib's first objection to situated criticism misses the mark.

Let me respond more briefly to Benhabib's second objection. She claims that situated criticism cannot account for cases in which a culture or society is so bad that the social critic is driven into exile (either literally or metaphorically). This objection is not persuasive, however, since it is not a true counterexample. When the exiled critic leaves her country, she doesn't go without any cultural baggage; she goes, rather, as a culturally formed and culturally situated critic. This was the situation of exiles from the Third Reich, arguably the worst society in human history. It was also, until recently, the situation of exiled members of the African National Congress, who left South Africa but took with them a complex culture of resistance comprising elements of Marxism, democratic theory, Christianity, and African values. Even the lone exile is a member of a community of the imagination and thus is also a situated critic.

I remain convinced, therefore, that social criticism without philosophy *is* possible, if we mean by "philosophy" what Linda Nicholson and I meant, namely, ahistorical, transcendental discourse claiming to articulate the criteria of validity for all other discourses. Nothing in this view precludes that the situated feminist critic is a radical critic, nor that she engages in critical self-clarification. Thus, what Benhabib considered irreconcilable ideas are reconcilable after all.

In general, Benhabib has unnecessarily polarized the debate by positing a set of false antitheses: antifoundationalism versus political engagement, situated criticism versus critical self-reflection, situated criticism versus radical opposition to one's society. Consequently, she has constructed a scenario in which she must reject poststructuralism altogether if she is to defend Critical Theory. However, since the wholesale rejection of poststructuralist ideas is neither theoretically defensible nor politically sound, the result is to provoke an equally one-sided poststructuralist riposte that jeopardizes the insights of Critical Theory.

This brings me to Judith Butler's paper, which presses an unnecessarily polarizing argument from the opposite direction. Butler's is a provocative paper, which displays her characteristic genius for insubordination. Seeking to rebut the frequently bruited charge that postmodernism is politically disabling for feminism, she questions the existence of postmodernism as anything other than a fevered figment of foundationalist paranoia. Thus, she turns the tables on her antagonists by suggesting that they have constructed a straw person in order to whip up support for an ailing and untenable foundationalist project. She claims that far from undermining feminist commitments, poststructuralist views of subjectivity, identity, and human agency enable and promote them.

Like Benhabib, Butler seeks to disaggregate the analytically distinct claims that are often lumped together under the labels "postmodernism" and "poststructuralism." Thus, although she doesn't herself use these terms, she, too, can be read as distinguishing weak and strong versions of such claims in order to defend a poststructuralist feminism that escapes the critics' objections. Butler is especially interested in countering the charge, endorsed by Benhabib, that the poststructuralist view of the subject undermines feminism by rendering it inconceivable that anyone could criticize, resist, or act to change their society. Moreover, the objection continues, even if poststructuralist theory could account for individual agency, its relentless nominalism and anti-essentialism would evacuate and delegitimate the category "women," thereby undermining the basis of female solidarity and of feminist movements.

In seeking to rebut these objections, Butler simultaneously provides a rejoinder to Benhabib's discussion of "the death of man." Recall that Benhabib distinguished two interpretations of this thesis: a weak version, which holds that the subject is situated in relation to a social, cultural, and discursive context; and a strong version, which holds that the subject is merely another position in language. Benhabib argued that only the weak version is compatible with feminism. In a direct reference to Butler's 1990 book, Benhabib asks: If we are no more than the sum total of gendered performances, how can we possibly rewrite the script?[11] Butler's paper can be read as an extended answer to this question. She seeks to show how a subject that is "merely" a discursive position can indeed rewrite the script.

In order to clarify what is at stake in this dispute, I shall distinguish and treat separately two sorts of claims—ontological and normative—that are intermingled in Butler's argument. I begin with the ontological. In her paper, Butler elaborates a poststructuralist ontology of the subject. She claims, *pace* Benhabib, that it is not sufficient to view the subject as *situated* vis-à-vis a setting or context that is external to it. Instead, we should see the subject as *constituted* in and through power/discourse formations. It follows that there exists no structure of subjectivity that is not always already an effect of a power/discourse matrix; there is no "ontologically intact reflexivity," no reflexivity that is not itself culturally constructed.

It is clear from her paper that Butler also believes that people have what I shall call "critical capacities"; we are not pre-programmed pawns but are able to engage in novel actions and to modify social conditions. Thus, I take her point here to be that critical capacities are culturally constructed. If that is right, one way of focusing her dispute with Benhabib is around the question, Where do critical capacities come from? Butler suggests that critics of poststructuralism like Benhabib treat critical capacities as a priori ontological structures of subjectivity, "ontologically intact," as opposed to culturally constructed. Benhabib's paper does not address this issue, and I am unsure whether she really holds that view.[12] In any case, there is no need for feminist theorists to hold it. On the contrary, it is perfectly possible to give an account of the cultural construction of critical capacities. Thus, nothing in principle precludes that subjects are *both* culturally constructed *and* capable of critique.

Suppose, therefore, we leave aside the question, Where do critical capacities come from in the past? Suppose we ask instead, What do they look like in the present? And how can we best characterize their future-directedness, the ways in which they point beyond their matrices of constitution? Here it is important to note that Butler's idiom privileges linguistic metaphors. She characterizes the subject as a "site of resignification" and a "permanent possibility of a certain resignifying process." This is her way of saying that the culturally constructed subject can rewrite the script. Thus, although the subject is itself the product of prior signifying processes, it is capable of *re*signification. Moreover, according to Butler, the subject as a site of resignification represents "power's own possibility of being reworked."

Let me make two observations about Butler's language. First, it is deeply antihumanist. What I have been referring to as "people's capacities" she describes as "power's own possibility" and as an impersonal "signifying process." This idiom is far enough removed from our everyday ways of talking and thinking about ourselves to require some justification. Why should we use such a self-distancing idiom? What are its theoretical advantages (and disadvantages)? What is its likely political impact? In the absence of any attention to these issues, Butler's paper at times projects an aura of esotericism unredeemed by any evident gains.

Second, in Butler's usage the term "resignification" carries a strong, if implicit, positive charge. In this respect, "resignification" functions in her discourse as "critique" has been functioning in mine. But in another respect the two terms differ sharply. "Critique" is logically connected to the concepts of warrant and justification, so its positive connotations are rooted in a claim to validity. This is not the case, however, with "resignification." Since Butler's term carries no implication of validity or warrant, its positive connotations are puzzling. Why is resignification good? Can't there be bad (oppressive, reactionary) resignifications? In opting for the epistemically neutral "resignification," as opposed to the epistemically positive "critique," Butler seems to valorize change for its own sake and thereby to disempower feminist judgment.

This brings me to the second set of claims implicit in Butler's poststructuralist account of subjectivity—normative, as opposed to ontological, claims. Such claims arise, first, in relation to the social practices through which subjects are constituted. Here Butler follows Foucault in claiming that practices of subjectivation are also practices of subjection. Like him, she insists that subjects are constituted through exclusion; some people are authorized to speak authoritatively because others are silenced. Thus, in Butler's view, the constitution of a class of authorized subjects entails "the creation of a domain of deauthorized subjects, pre-subjects, figures of abjection, populations erased from view."

But is it really the case that no one can become the subject of speech without others' being silenced? Are there no counterexamples? Where such exclusions do exist, are they all bad? Are they all equally bad? Can we distinguish legitimate from illegitimate exclusions, better from worse practices of subjectivation? Is subject-authorization *inherently* a zero-sum game? Or does it only become one in oppressive societies? Can we overcome or at least ameliorate the asymmetries in current practices of subjectivation? Can we construct practices, institutions, and forms of life in which the empowerment of some does not entail the disempowerment of others? If not, what is the point of feminist struggle?

Butler offers no help in thinking about these issues. Nor can she, I submit, so long as she fails to integrate critical-theoretical considerations into her poststructuralist Foucauldian framework. That framework, I have argued elsewhere, is structurally incapable of providing satisfactory answers to the normative questions it unfailingly solicits.[13] It needs modification and supplementation, therefore, in order to be fully adequate to the feminist project.

In addition to her claims about the social practices of subjectivation, Butler also makes normative claims about the relative merits of different *theories* of subjectivity. She claims that some such theories are "politically insidious," whereas others are progressive or emancipatory. On the insidious side is the view of subjectivity as possessing an ontologically intact reflexivity that is not an effect of cultural processes of subjectivation. This view, according to Butler, is a "ruse of power" and an "instrument of cultural imperialism."

Is it really? There is no denying that foundationalist theories of subjectivity have often functioned as instruments of cultural imperialism. But is that due to conceptual necessity or historical contingency? In fact, there are cases where such theories have had emancipatory effects—witness the French Revolution and the appropriation of its foundationalist view of subjectivity by the Haitian "Black Jacobin," Toussaint de l'Ouverture.[14] These examples show that it is not possible to deduce a single, univocal political valence from a theory of subjectivity. Such theories, too, are bits of cultural discourse whose meanings are subject to "resignification."[15]

How, then, should we resolve the Benhabib-Butler dispute over "the death of man"? I conclude that Butler is right in maintaining that a culturally constructed subject can also be a critical subject, but that the terms in which she formulates the point give rise to difficulties. Specifically, "resignification" is not an adequate substitute for "critique," since it surrenders the normative moment. Likewise, the view that subjectivation necessarily entails subjection precludes normative distinctions between better and worse subjectivating practices. Finally, the view that foundationalist theories of subjectivity are inherently oppressive is historically disconfirmed, and it is conceptually incompatible with a contextualist theory of meaning. The upshot, then, is that feminists need to develop an alternative conceptualization of the subject, one that integrates Butler's poststructuralist emphasis on construction with Benhabib's critical-theoretical stress on critique.

Let me turn briefly to Butler's discussion of the problem of "women" in feminist theory. She provides an account of the processes by which American feminists' descriptions of women have functioned covertly as prescriptions, thereby provoking protest and factionalization within the movement. Butler maintains that these processes exemplify an inescapable logic. On the one hand, feminist movements cannot avoid making claims in the name of "women"; on the other, the category "women" that is constructed via those claims is necessarily subject to continual deconstruction. Butler concludes that feminists should view this dialectic not as a political disaster but as a political resource. We should prize the fact that "women" "designates an undesignatable field of differences . . . that cannot be totalized or summarized by a descriptive identity category."[16]

What should we make of this discussion? For the most part I find
Butler's account illuminating and apt. I am persuaded by her claim
that the self-deconstructing tendencies within feminism are endemic
to identity movements and cannot be eliminated by fiat. But I am not
convinced of the merits of her conclusion. The idea of "women" or
"woman" as the sign of an untotalizable field of differences is suscep-
tible to two interpretations, one strong and indefensible, the other
weak and uninteresting. The strong thesis is the one associated with
French feminist theory, according to which "woman" cannot be
defined but signifies difference and non-identity. This, of course, is a
paradoxical claim, since to make "woman" the sign of the undefin-
able is thereby precisely to define it. Moreover, this (anti-)definition
is mystifying. Why should "woman" or "women" be the sign of the
non-identical? Isn't everything Butler says about "women" also true
of "men," "workers," "people of color," "Chicanos," or any collective nomination? There is no privileged relation between the appella-
tion "women" and what is actually the general political problem of
how to construct cultures of solidarity that are not homogenizing
and repressive.[17]

A more defensible interpretation of Butler's suggestion would follow the Fraser-Nicholson view discussed earlier. According to this
view, generalizing claims about "women" are inescapable but always
subject to revision; they should be advanced nonfoundationally and
fallibilistically. Further, the assumptions underlying such claims should
be genealogized, framed by contextualizing narrative and rendered
culturally and historically specific.[18]

Although this interpretation of Butler's claim is defensible, it still
does not address the underlying political problem. That problem,
which is dissimulated in Butler's discussion, is whether there are real
conflicts of interest among women of different classes, ethnicities,
nationalities, and sexual orientations, conflicts so intractable as not
to be harmonizable, or even finessable, within feminist movements.
Certainly, there *are* conflicts when interests are defined relative to
present forms of social organization; an example is the clash in
interests between professional white middle class First World
women and the Third World women of color they employ as domestic workers. In the face of this sort of conflict, uncritical, celebratory
talk about women's "differences" is a mystification. The hard question feminist movements need to face is one Butler's proposal elides:
Can "we" envision new social arrangements that would harmonize

present conflicts? And if so, can "we" articulate "our" vision in terms that are sufficiently compelling to persuade other women—and men —to reinterpret their interests?

Butler's essay misses those questions, I think, because of the inadequacy of her conception of liberation. At the deepest level, she understands women's liberation as liberation *from* identity, since she views identity as inherently oppressive. It follows that deconstructive critique—critique that dereifies or unfreezes identity—is the privileged mode of feminist theorizing, whereas normative, reconstructive critique is normalizing and oppressive. But this view is far too one-sided to meet the full needs of a liberatory politics. Feminists *do* need to make normative judgments and to offer emancipatory alternatives. We are not for "anything goes." Moreover, it is arguable that the current proliferation of identity-dereifying, fungible, commodified images and significations constitutes as great a threat to women's liberation as do fixed, fundamentalist identities. In fact, dereifying processes and reifying processes are two sides of the same postfordist coin. They demand a two-sided response. Feminists need both deconstruction *and* reconstruction, destabilization of meaning *and* projection of utopian hope.

I conclude that Butler, too, has generated a series of false antitheses: identity versus difference, subjectivation versus reciprocity, dereification versus normative critique, deconstruction versus reconstruction. She, too, has unnecessarily polarized the debate by insinuating that feminists face an either/or choice between Critical Theory and poststructuralism.

It is unfortunate that Benhabib and Butler should finally find common ground in subscribing to a false antithesis between Critical Theory and poststructuralism. By framing their debate in such dichotomous terms, they miss the chance to try another, more promising tack. I have suggested that instead of assuming we must choose between these two approaches, we might reformulate the claims of each so as to render them mutually compatible. Thus, instead of clinging to a series of mutually reinforcing false antitheses, we might conceive subjectivity as endowed with critical capacities *and* as culturally constructed. Similarly, we might view critique as simultaneously situated *and* amenable to self-reflection, as potentially radical *and* subject to warrants. Likewise, we might posit a relation to history that is at once antifoundationalist *and* politically engaged, while promoting a field of multiple historiographies that is both contextualized *and* provisionally totalizing. Finally, we might develop a view of collective identities as at once discursively constructed *and* complex, enabling of collective action *and* amenable to mystification, in need of deconstruction *and* reconstruction. In sum, we might try to develop new paradigms of feminist theorizing that integrate the insights of Critical Theory with the insights of poststructuralism. Such paradigms would yield important intellectual and political gains, while finally laying to rest the false antitheses of our current debates.

Notes

1. I am grateful for helpful comments from Thomas McCarthy, Linda Nicholson, and Eli Zaretsky. The papers discussed here are Seyla Benhabib, "Feminism and the Question of Postmodernism" and Judith Butler, "Contingent Foundations: Feminism and the Question of 'Postmodernism,'" both in this volume.

2. The paradigm case of teleological Marxian metanarrative is Georg Lukacs's view of the proletariat as the subject-object of history in *History and Class Consciousness*, tr. Rodney Livingstone (Merlin, 1971). For a critique of Marxian metanarrative in the name of postmodernism, see Jean-François Lyotard, *The Postmodern Condition: A Report on Knowledge*, tr. G. Bennington and B. Massumi (University of Minnesota Press, 1984). For a more extreme view, which threatens to evacuate history altogether, see Jean Baudrillard, *Simulations* (Semiotext(e), 1983). For a recent neoconservative appropriation of the death of history theme, see Francis Fukuyama, "The End of History?" *The National Interest* (Summer 1989) pp. 3–18. All of these critics fail to consider alternative versions and aspects of Marxism that do not rely on teleological metanarrative.

3. Nancy Fraser and Linda J. Nicholson, "Social Criticism without Philosophy: An Encounter between Feminism and Postmodernism," *Theory, Culture & Society*, vol. 5, nos. 2–3 (1988) pp. 373–394. Reprinted in *Feminism and Postmodernism*, ed. Linda Nicholson (Routledge, Chapman and Hall, 1989) pp. 19–38.

4. Examples of such large narratives are Linda J. Nicholson, *Gender and History: The Limits of Social Theory in the Age of the Family* (Columbia University Press, 1986) and Eli Zaretsky, *Capitalism, the Family and Personal Life* (Harper & Row, 1986).

5. Thomas McCarthy has suggested an alternative interpretation. Perhaps Benhabib's claim is that large-scale histories cannot be sharply distinguished from metanarratives since they utilize general categories. That view assumes that general categories cannot also be categories whose status is nonfoundational. Thus it too posits a false antithesis. I discuss this issue below in the context of Benhabib's treatment of "the death of metaphysics."

6. Among the many examples I could cite are Linda Gordon, *Heroes of Their Own Lives: The Politics and History of Family Violence, Boston 1880–1960* (Penguin Books, 1988); Carroll Smith-Rosenberg, "The Female World of Love and Ritual: Relations Between Women in 19th Century America," *Signs: Journal of Women in Culture and Society*, vol. 1, no. 1 (1975) pp. 1–29; and Joan Wallach Scott, *Gender and the Politics of History* (Columbia University Press, 1988).

7. Benhabib's rejection of situated social criticism is especially puzzling in the light of her endorsement of a theory of the situated subject. (See Seyla Benhabib, *Situating the Self: Gender, Community and Postmodernism in Contemporary Ethics* [New York: Routledge, 1992].) One might think that the two went together, since it is not clear how a situated subject could produce unsituated criticism. I discuss the question of the situated subject below.

8. Michael Walzer, *Spheres of Justice: A Defense of Pluralism and Equality* (Basic Books, 1983).

9. As it does in the case of John Rawls, for example. Rawls provides a good example of an approach that retains a high level of conceptual abstraction and generality even while acknowledging its own situatedness. Thus, he has interpreted his general theorizing about justice as an attempt to seek "reflective equilibrium." See Rawls, "Kantian Constructivism in Moral Theory," *Journal of Philosophy*, vol. 77 (1980).

10. My own view is that contextualizing historical narrative is often more useful than abstract conceptual analysis. Insofar as "pure" conceptual reflection, untainted by empirical content, undertakes to justify principles of, say, democracy and equality, it trades in relatively uncontroversial abstractions and sidesteps the hard questions about how to apply such principles in social life. *Those* questions are more fruitfully addressed via "impure" interdisciplinary efforts integrating normative and empirical considerations. But this kind of empirical-cum-normative reflection is not sharply separated from first-order social criticism; it is the latter's immanent self-clarification.

11. The reference is to Butler's book, *Gender Trouble: Feminism and the Subversion of Identity* (Routledge, Chapman and Hall, 1990), which elaborates a performative theory of gender.

12. Benhabib certainly rejects the self-authorizing subject of instrumental reason, which Butler evokes in the her discussion of American militarism and the Gulf War. On this point, there is no disagreement between them. Neither Butler nor Benhabib defends a theory of the self-authorizing subject that could entirely master its milieu. Both agree that that is a masculinist "fantasy of autogenesis" predicated on a disavowal or repression of "feminine" dependence.

13. Nancy Fraser, "Foucault on Modern Power: Empirical Insights and Normative Confusions," *Praxis International*, vol. 1, no. 3 (October 1981) pp. 272–287. Reprinted in Nancy Fraser, *Unruly Practices: Power, Discourse and Gender in Contemporary Social Theory* (University of Minnesota Press and Polity Press, 1989).

14. See C. R. L. James, *The Black Jacobins* (1938).

15. I develop a more extensive version of this argument in "Foucault's Body-Language: A Post-Humanist Political Rhetoric?" in Fraser, *Unruly Practices. op. cit.*

16. Here Butler seems close to Theodor Adorno's attempt to articulate a non-identitarian mode of thinking, although she does not share his focus on reconciliation. See Adorno, *Negative Dialectics*, tr. E. B. Ashton (Continuum Press, 1973).

17. For critical discussion of French feminist theories of "woman" as sign of non-identity, see Nancy Fraser, "The Uses and Abuses of French Discourse Theories for Feminist Politics," in *Revaluing French Feminism: Critical Essays on Difference, Agency, and Culture*, ed. Nancy Fraser and Sandra Bartky (Indiana University Press, 1991). See also my "Introduction" to that volume.

18. This point is elaborated in Fraser and Nicholson, "Social Criticism Without Philosophy," *op. cit.*

4

What Is Ethical Feminism?

Drucilla Cornell

I. Introduction

My purpose in this essay is to summarize what I mean by ethical feminism. I will proceed as follows: First, I will define the sense in which I use the word "ethical" in the context of feminism. Second, I will specify my use of psychoanalysis, particularly as I rely on and yet also critique and re-elaborate certain key concepts of the psychoanalytic framework provided by Jacques Lacan. As I hope to show, this re-elaboration is inspired by a feminist purpose. There is a theoretical need to understand how the symbolic constructions we know as Woman are inseparable from the way in which fantasies of femininity are unconsciously "colored" and imagined within the constraints of gender hierarchy and the norms of so-called heterosexuality. I write "so-called," because it is crucial to my critique of gender hierarchy that gender hierarchy restricts the elaboration of the feminine within sexual difference by its reduction of the feminine to what is not man. A crucial aspect of ethical feminism is that it enlarges continually the space in which we could both write and speak of the rich and multi-layered sexuality of a creature that struggles to achieve individuation from the imposed strictures of gender hierarchy and rigid gender identity. Such a creature would remain as other, the *heteros* to a system of gender hierarchy which thwarts the process and the struggle for individuation. The frame of psychoanalysis I use challenges other psychoanalytic, as well as sociological and historical approaches, that investigate gender as separable from race, class, nationality, and sanctioned heterosexuality. Such approaches frequently fail to grapple with the infection of racial and sexual stereotypes in the definitions of femininity that unconsciously inform the questions that are asked in social-scientific investigations and policy recommendations.[1] As feminists, we need to investigate the complex interplay between fantasies of Woman and the material oppression of women. Such an investigation would demand that we open up the meaning of referentiality. I would never deny that there "are" women and that those of us who are so designated suffer as women, as objects of rape and sexual abuse and as victims of economic discrimination. But if we are to come to terms with the reality of this oppression we will have to alter our conception of the meaning of referentiality. Psychoanalysis can aid in effecting this alteration by providing us with analytic tools which may enable a critique of the way in which social reality is engendered by unconscious fantasies.

I will also give an account of the significance of my understanding of the limit of any system of meaning, including a theory of justice and of gender identity[2] which attempts to fully justify itself and which posits what can be realistically imagined.[3] It was Wittgenstein who tirelessly and brilliantly showed us that meaning is bounded only by a form of life and that those bounds can be loosened as we struggle against the constraints of convention, expand our sensibility, and re-imagine our form of life.[4] The Wittgensteinian insight that the limits of language are the limits of our world has frequently been misread as a bar to the imagination because this limit is understood to secure meaning and thus give us the world as we know it as "ours."[5] In fact, language as a limit recedes as we try to philosophically defend it as a boundary that can be known. The central insight of Wittgenstein was to demonstrate the paradox inherent in the operation of our language as a limit; one that both gives us our world and yet keeps us from being imprisoned in it. From within a very different tradition, Jacques Derrida makes a similar demonstration but with the explicit thematization of the recognition of how attempts to reinscribe the limit as a bar are informed by phallic metaphors.[6] Thus, he describes such efforts as phallogocentrism. We are, therefore, returned to the significance of psychoanalysis as an analytic and critical tool that uncovers the laws of a masculine symbolic as the basis for the philosophical defense of the limit of language.

I have argued that it is a serious mistake to identify what has come to be known as deconstruction with irrationalism.[7] Nor do I find the word "post-modernism" useful in helping us understand what is at stake in recent philosophical debates.[8] Indeed, the labeling process has served as a *pharmakon*,[9] both "curing" and "poisoning" our minds by closing them to the important ethical and political issues that are advanced by re-thinking the significance of the limit of the symbolic order, of the world structured not only by conventional meaning but by the fantasies that give body and weight to our form of life. The feminist alliance with this philosophical project is that it brings us beyond our current system of gender identity, beyond the restrictive dictates which we can too easily take for granted as the necessary basis for civilization and the inevitable constraint of the nature of "man."[10]

Central then to the debate presented in this book is the place of both the imagination and what has been traditionally thought as the aesthetic in feminist politics. I have argued elsewhere that feminism involves an apotropaic gesture against the incessant fading of the diversification and differentiation of the feminine within sexual difference and within cultural representations.[11] I now want to emphasize that this apotropaic gesture is crucial to the day-to-day political struggles of feminism.[12] The struggle to re-symbolize the feminine within sexual difference beyond the restrictive figures of Woman which simplistically divide actual women into two kinds, good girls, loving mothers, adoring and nonthreatening sisters on the one hand, and manipulative mistresses, suffocating mothers, man-hating lesbians, and psychotic drop-outs on the other, is crucial to a feminist effort at a solidarity that respects difference and grapples with privilege. This psychical fantasy of Woman[13] too easily divides women from one another as some of us pass ourselves off as "good girls," implicitly promising to remain a non-disruptive presence within the civilized order of "man."[14] It should be obvious that this possibility of passing is more readily available to white, middle-class women than it is to women of color. It should not be surprising then that this process of splitting and passing has taken its toll on the development and sustenance of academic feminism. The appeal to an established and shared identity as women can obscure the significance of this often unconscious process of splitting and passing. As we will see, in the place of an appeal to identity as the basis of politics, I rely instead on what I refer to as an explicitly political enactment of mimetic identification as the basis for solidarity.

It is the dearth of symbolizations of the feminine within sexual difference that yields the experience of silencing often testified to in feminist literature. Feminism, as a result, cannot be separated from "the words to say it."[15] The "it" is not only the articulation of the experience of being pushed against the limit of meaning as an actual woman struggling with and against the restrictive femininity imposed by the gender hierarchy.[16] The "it" also involves the re-imagining and the re-articulation of the most basic concepts of Western philosophy and jurisprudence so as to elaborate a feminist practice that does not turn against its own aspirations by accommodating to the terms of the gender hierarchy that it challenges.

II. Why Ethical Feminism?

The use I make of the word "ethical" is multi-layered. For purposes of this essay I will attempt a summation of what I have defended in much greater depth elsewhere.[17] I use the word "ethical" to indicate the aspiration to a nonviolent relationship to the Other and to otherness in the widest possible sense. This assumes responsibility to struggle against the appropriation of the Other into any system of meaning that would deny her difference and singularity.[18] Since the emphasis is on the aspiration to a nonviolent relationship to the Other, such a definition of the ethical demands that we pay attention to what kind of person we must become in order to aspire to a nonviolative relationality. I separate this aspiration, along with the aspiration to transform oneself, from any attempt to determine morality. For my purposes, morality designates any attempt to theoretically spell out how one determines a system that absolutely governs the "right way to behave." As Niklas Luhmann has succinctly defined it, "morality is a special form of communication which carries within it indications of approval or disapproval."[19] The ethical as I define it is not a system of behavioral rules, nor a system of positive standards by which to justify disapproval of others. It is, rather, an attitude towards what is other to oneself. This attitude shares much in common with those which Charles Peirce called fallibilism and musement.[20] Fallibilism implies a challenge to one's basic organization of the world, while musement indicates the stance of amazement before the mysteries and marvels of life. The attitudes of fallibilism and musement are interrelated. In one sense, I am using ethical as opposed to moral in a very traditional manner since these two attitudes could be translated into specific virtues, for example humility and generosity. But on my understanding of the limits of a theoretical reflection on morality, this translation would not be within the tradition of an ethics that elaborates the virtues within a description of a normative-rational sphere of nature. The ethical as I understand it *should not* be grasped as a determinable, theoretical reflection of morality. The purpose of such a theoretical reflection is to elaborate a pure view of practical reason. The irony is that such a theoretical reflection can itself become intolerant, thus defeating its purpose of elaborating a practical defense of the virtue of public reason. Intolerance is clearly incompatible with that virtue. Thus, I argue that *ethically,* as well as philosophically, we should not attempt the theoretical defense of the pure view of practical reason. I prefer, instead, to describe fallibilism and musement as attitudes.

These attitudes would make one wary of the potential connection between proscriptive judgements, particularly as these enact rules of encoded behavior and become the "market of approval."[21] As feminists we make and need to make such judgments all the time, but the attitudes I have described and attributed to the aspiration to the ethical relationship would make one suspicious of any attempt to combine our judgments into a system of moral integration—even one we purportedly justify on the basis of a theoretical reflection on morality.[22] Importantly, this suspicion of the theoretical development of a system of moral integration is not based on Nietzsche's critique of morality.[23] Nietzsche would certainly not endorse the aspiration to a nonviolent relation to the Other. For him such an aspiration would be an indicator of the worst kind of insipid "sissiness." A fully determinable morality, nevertheless, risks a collapse into the "market of approval" that will always exclude the crucial task of re-imagining our own standards of right and wrong.

Feminism presents this kind of endless challenge to the ethical imagination. Feminists are continually calling on all of us to re-imagine our forms of life. We demand that harms that were traditionally understood as part of the inevitable behavior of "boys will be boys," such as date rape and sexual harassment, be recognized as serious wrongs to women. In order to make these behaviors appear as wrongs, feminists struggle to make us "see" the world differently. The debate over what kind of behavior constitutes sexual harassment turns on how the legal system "sees" women and men. Because feminism is a call for us to re-imagine our form of life so that we can "see" differently, it necessarily involves an ethical appeal, including an appeal to expand our moral sensibility. A sensibility informed by the attitudes of fallibilism and musement will be more likely to respond to such an appeal.

It is through this sensibility that feminists are allied with the ethical critique of *theoretical* attempts to secure a system of moral integration through the elaboration of a pure view of practical reason. Please note that I am not denying the obvious: we, without a doubt, need principles. We need to develop the best possible definition of the harm to women in sexual harassment so that it can be effectively comprehended as a legally addressable claim. We need to be able to explain why such behavior is wrong and why our concept of right is what makes it wrong. But we also need to be open to the revision of these concepts as we engage in the arduous process of re-imagining our form of life. The dispute then is not over whether we need rights, and correspondingly whether there are principles of right and wrong, but whether or not there can be a *theoretical* reflection of morality that can give us the last word on the Right in the strong Kantian sense. The specific addition here is that the very attempt to give us the last word through a theoretical reflection on morality would be ethically suspect under the definition I have given. I need to stress that this suspicion should not be understood to be directed against experiments in the hypothetical imagination, such as the representational device of the "veil of ignorance."[24] We need such representational devices in the elaboration of principles of justice. The dispute would begin only if such experiments in the hypothetical imagination attempt to ground themselves in theoretical rather than practical reason. The attempt to justify the pure view of practical reason necessarily grounds itself in a *theoretical* justification of what would constitute the pure view.

I want to emphasize this point because, as I've argued elsewhere, I believe that there is an important and timely alliance that must be made between feminism and John Rawls's theory of justice.[25] For my purposes here, I want to note that Rawls's project explicitly rejects the description of a normative rational sphere of nature as inappropriate to the elaboration of a project of justice guided primarily by practical reason. It is precisely Rawls's insistence that one cannot theoretically justify a pure view of practical reason that makes his work an ally of what I am calling "ethical feminism." It is, of course, beyond the scope of this essay, to develop in detail the outlines of this alliance. But since the essays in this book take up the question of the relationship between so called "post-modernism" and Kantianism, I do want to engage this debate by stressing that I believe that this divide has not been correctly described by the other contributors in this volume. Instead, we need to examine, in much more detail, the basis for an alliance with feminism and Kantianism as it is developed in the work of John Rawls's theory of justice.[26] But two aspects of Rawls's project serve as the necessary underpinnings for such an alliance. The first, as I've already indicated, is his Peircean insistence that a theory of justice must primarily rely on standards of objectivity and reasonableness appropriate to the sphere of practical and not theoretical reason. For instance, Rawls explicitly rejects the introduction into debates guided by practical reason of theories of causal appropriateness as these inform theoretical accounts of objectivity. A classic example of the introduction of a theory of causal appropriateness into an account of practical reason is Habermas's attempt to incorporate Kolberg's cognitive psychology into his theoretical justification of a dialogic conception of justice.[27] Rawls, on the other hand, correctly argues that we should not and cannot borrow from theoretical concepts of objectivity and incorporate them into the field of practical reason we call justice.[28]

The second crucial aspect is, because of his great care to enumerate exactly what public reason can or cannot cover, that Rawls does not defend traditional Kantian distinctions between the aesthetic and the ethical—at least as the basis for a philosophical foregrounding of a theory of justice or his conception of political liberalism.[29] This care to avoid any defense of Kantian metaphysics as it particularly turns on a defense of the divide between the aesthetic and the ethical is crucial to ethical feminism because ethical feminism turns us to what has traditionally been called the aesthetic, in order to fill out and make vivid our conception of wrongs women suffer when they are, for example, denied the right of abortion or forced to endure sexually harassing behavior.[30]

Rawls's work, then, can and should be understood as consistent with the kind of Peircean pragmatism I have advocated as the basis for giving us workable definitions in objectivity and reason as they should be defined by the parameters of a particular field.[31] The call, then, is to be modest before the very claims of theoretical reason that have so often been used to attempt to ground theories of justice. I am using the word "modest" deliberately because the "veil of ignorance" itself is a powerful, metaphoric reminder of the two aspects of modesty associated with the veil. The first is sexual shame. The second is an important twist on the very idea of modesty . . . no, not modesty imposed upon women by cultures in which their sex is degraded and devalued and therefore found shameful, but the modesty imposed upon us by the dictates of justice itself. Although I'm well aware that the "veil of ignorance" was not deliberately tailored to play out these two aspects of modesty, the power and the beauty of the representational device is inseparable from this very twist. The call, in the second sense, to modesty, before any attempts at theoretical reason and the theoretical elaboration of gender, is important as a warning against the self-righteousness that has too frequently informed brands of feminism that have insisted on theoretical correctness.

In like manner, this ethical suspicion of any attempt to develop a strong philosophical defense of any current system of morality also plays an important role within feminism itself. It does so in at least two ways: First, the ethical suspicion serves as a reminder against the danger of the "market of approval" within feminism. Of course, there are examples of moralizing which purportedly divide the righteous feminists from those women who have fallen prey to false consciousness and who disagree on a given position enunciated by a self-defined feminist. One glaring example is Catharine MacKinnon's accusation that feminists who disagree with her position on pornography are collaborators.[32] MacKinnon has herself argued that the feminist methodology is consciousness raising.[33] But unless one argues that there is a truth prior to consciousness raising—and MacKinnon vacillates about whether or not there is such a truth—then there is no such thing as a consciousness raised once and for all so that those with that consciousness can show us "the one True Way."[34]

In contrast to MacKinnon, I believe consciousness raising does not involve the revelation of our ultimate situation as women. Rather, I understand consciousness raising as the endless attempt to re-imagine and re-symbolize the feminine within sexual difference so as to break the bonds of the meanings of Woman that have been taken for granted and that have been justifiable as fate. The attitudes of fallibilism and musement are crucial for the trust and solidarity necessary for the process of challenging the strictures of femininity and re-presenting ourselves beyond the stereotypes of femininity. Consciousness raising engages the meaning of representation on at least two levels. First, the truth that arises out of consciousness raising, if it does arise, is representative, in that it represents a view of the world that has come to be shared by the group. Second, such a truth involves a representation of reality, particularly of the strictures of gender identity, so that what has faded can be drawn into vivid outlines, what has been invisible can be seen, what seemed natural can be challenged and imagined differently. On this level, consciousness raising involves an apotropaic gesture that operates against the sedimentation of gender identity into an unshakable reality.

There is a second, more subtle form of moralizing that is perhaps even more corrosive of feminist solidarity. That form of moralizing involves the separation, undertaken by feminists themselves, between a sensible feminism committed to a reasonable program of reform, and the "wild" feminism that seems to leave little of our most basic institutional practices unchallenged. This kind of moralizing can be found in the disassociation of some feminists from the struggle for the equal citizenship of gays and lesbians. Since I agree with Judith Butler on how one comes to have a "sex," it is a theoretical as well as an ethical mistake to try to separate gender from the matrix of heterosexuality.[35] But for now I wish to emphasize the ethical dimension of this attempt at separation. A characteristic of this kind of moralizing is that it reinscribes the psychical fantasy of Woman which splits women into two, the "tamed" and the "wild." If feminism sets out to challenge the reigning symbolic order of gender hierarchy, then it ironically reinforces it if it succumbs to the fantasy that there can be a "good" feminism and a "bad" feminism. This division relies on a form of splitting, as I outlined earlier, that is imposed upon us by the dearth of symbolizations of the feminine within sexual difference. To put oneself on one side or the other not only legitimizes the fantasy that this split is "true" of Woman, it also effectuates a split that undermines any attempt at solidarity.

Once we understand that solidarity is not just given to us on the basis of our shared identity as women we—and by we I mean feminists—are returned to our responsibility for perpetuating fissures within feminism that replicate the psychical fantasy of Woman. I have already suggested that this divide is "colored" with the implication that it is much easier to pass as a "good girl" if one is white. There is a drawback, however, to having easier access to the position of the "good girl." As bell hooks reminds us, the very trappings of femininity—and I am using the words trappings deliberately—such as prettiness, serenity, understanding, undemanding care, and reliability, are whitened.[36] If by accommodating ourselves to the psychical fantasy of women we make ourselves more "attractive," and thus find it easier to pass into the established institutional structures, we also reinforce our own prisons by legitimating the strictures of femininity. The repudiation of femininity frequently associated with professional women replicates the stereotypes of femininity precisely because it is these stereotypes that are being repudiated as the truth of Woman. Repudiation cannot heal the wound of femininity because it reinstates it as the truth of Woman. The dichotomy between repudiation and accommodation, set up for example in the writing of Simone de Beauvoir, implicitly justifies the myth of the superiority of the woman of class and creativity who escapes her identification with the "second sex."[37] In the case of de Beauvoir, however, the myth of her escape entrapped her more deeply as the femininity she repudiated clung to her in the form of its very denial.[38] In psychoanalytic terms this repudiation is itself a form of symbolic castration.

Yet, if there is an oppressiveness associated with these often unconscious strategies of accommodation and repudiation, it should not be understood to deny the race and class privilege upon which these strategies depend and which they re-inscribe. The divisions within feminism demand that we confront both difference and *privilege*, including privilege we may unconsciously take on as we pass into established institutional structures and thus seemingly move away from our situation as women.[39]

How can we take responsibility for what is unconscious? There is a paradox here, but it is a paradox that inheres in feminism. Feminism challenges all of us to try to come to terms with the damaging effects of the unconscious fantasies that give body to gender hierarchy. As I have argued, ethical feminism demands that the philosophical thinking of the ethical relation confront the way in which it is informed and framed by the psychical fantasy of Woman.[40] The very process of consciousness raising demands that we struggle to make unconscious patterns conscious without by definition knowing that we are succeeding or being authentic. It is the Other, including the other in ourselves, that calls us to this responsibility. As a result, we cannot develop standards which say "enough," for example, that we, as white feminists, can stop the struggle to come to terms with our own racism. Ironically, the development of rationalized moral standards are often used in just this way, to give us a reason for not heeding the call of the Other. Derrida has frequently made this point.[41] My own addition is that the ethical is more ruthlessly demanding of our own transformation than an established system of morality, since we cannot *theoretically* justify when or where we can stop the practice of consciousness raising.[42] The explicit call within feminism by women of color, lesbians, and others designated as outside the matrix of heterosexuality is that white, heterosexual women take responsibility for the way in which they internalize and act out the privileges of "passing."

This call to responsibility inheres in the aspiration to the ethical relationship and is as a result a crucial aspect of what I call ethical feminism. It can call us to both acts of identification and dis-identification. But it demands of us that we deconstruct the claim that there is an identity that we share as women and that the differences between us are secondary. A simple claim to identity obscures the way in which we as women are "read" differently and thus are "seen" differently within the reigning fantasies of femininity that give "body" to our "selves" as women. The ethical danger in this obscuration is that it disguises privilege. It is also out of accord with the apotropaic gesture that I have argued is crucial for a feminist practice because it obscures and reinforces the fading of the diversification and differentiation of the feminine within sexual difference. In a very important sense, I differentiate between psychoanalytic and other theoretical approaches to the study of Woman and women precisely on the basis of whether they serve us in making this apotropaic gesture. Let me turn now to my discussion of how and why I engage the theoretical framework of Jacques Lacan and why I am critical of certain aspects of the account of gender given by object-relations theory.

III. Why Lacan?

Many feminists have been wary of Lacan because his psychoanalytic framework seems to leave no room for feminism.[43] Not surprisingly, Lacan agreed. He argued that his analytic framework shut out the possibility of feminism which could radically challenge the very engendering of sexual difference into two genders. Why then engage such a thinker who emphasizes the most fundamental exclusion of the feminine as the "ground" for culture? The answer is that Lacanian analysis can help us in the development of an approach to the work of culture that allows us to plunge into the depths of our form of life, rather than simply skim along the surface. Lacan aids us in grappling with the way our reality is shaped by unconscious fantasies that severely restrict our field of vision and our political imagination.

I want to emphasize two aspects of Lacan's work which make his theorizing important to feminism and more specifically how it can account for the process by which the diversification of the feminine within sexual difference fades within cultural representations. Let me emphasize again that is precisely Lacan's explanation of the fading of the diversification of the feminine within sexual difference that makes his work an important starting point for understanding what the apotropaic gesture of feminism must operate against.

Let me summarize the two aspects of Lacan's work which are particularly crucial to feminist theory and practice. First, Lacanian analysis begins with the symbolic construction of femininity, an approach that never conflates the constructions with actual women and thus never relies on any empirical account of sexual difference. Why do I think it is important to begin with the conscious knowledge that one is examining the constructions of femininity and not just reporting on an obvious reality? The answer lies in the fact that there is always a gap between these constructions and the lives of actual women. As I have argued elsewhere, feminism functions within this gap, the space necessarily left open between the constructions and our actual lives as "sexed" creatures.[44] This gap—which for Lacan guarantees that there can be no telling of the truth of our sexual difference—can be interpreted against his own political repudiation of the possibility of feminism. The impossibility of a simply empirical description of our sexual difference means there is no truth to who we are as women. For Lacan, the fantasies and imagistic signifiers that yield the representations of Woman do not end in a ground for Woman in either biology or the roles allotted to her by social convention. That there is no ground that we can reach as a reality beyond the fantasy structures is what Lacan means when he writes that there is no fixed signified for Woman within the symbolic order.[45] We will return to why Lacan's analysis of how and why there is no ground for Woman leads him to his conclusions about feminism. I would like to stress, however, that in Lacanian terms we can re-interpret the political significance that there is no fixed signified for Woman within the masculine symbolic.

Lacanian analysis and the use of psychoanalysis in feminist theory does not deny there is a referent "women," but it does demand that we study how that referent has come "to be." We must delve into the fantasies that have become so much a part of us that we cannot imagine reality without them. Obviously race and its manifestation through unconscious associations with color has played a crucial role in how femininity is inscribed in a particular culture. The famous speech, "Ain't I a Woman," deliberately plays off the paradox inherent in a definition of femininity that systematically excluded the lives and destinies of African American women.[46]

In other words, my use of psychoanalysis does not give us a feminism without women. It gives us a feminism that provides us with a rich complex analysis of how the meaning of woman and women is unconsciously encoded and how the encoded meanings carry with them paradoxes that allow for the political challenge. Woman as the "lack" is one example of what I mean by an encoding paradox. If woman is lack, and thus, in Lacan's sense lacking meaning, she can "be" anything.[47] The impossibility of absolutely fixing the meaning of Woman yields endless transformative possibility. And because of this impossibility we can challenge any theory that supposedly imprisons us in the truth of our difference. We can also operate within the gap between these constructions and our actual lives and, consequently, open the space for the enactment of new choreographies of sexual difference. This approach is in contrast to the literal-mindedness of the approach that studies women as if the situation of women could be understood as a series of established facts. This understanding of sexual difference frequently leads to the "gender-and-" approach which has come under such severe criticism from some women of color. But it also rigidly designates what a woman is, itself a form of confinement. Like all confinements, it certainly does not fit with the lived diversity and difference of actual lives. The approach I offer to the work of culture insists that we are engendered as women in a complex structure of desire which colors us at the same time that it engenders us as sexed. Yet, it always does so imperfectly because there can be no stable analogy between cultural representations and lived experience.

The second aspect of Lacan's theory that I critically appropriate is his insight that it is the bar to the feminine within sexual difference that serves as the ground of culture. Lacanian analysis makes the figure of the castrated Mother the key to the castration complex. This understanding of the view of the mother in the castration complex means that it is how the mother is seen, and not the presence or involvement of fathers, that is crucial to shifting the basis of gender identity, and particularly in militating against the depressive symptoms that girls demonstrate at such an early age.[48] The emphasis on the damaging effects of the lack of the father or correspondingly the significance given to identification with the father for individuation is implicitly challenged. This view of psychoanalysis which idealizes the power of the actual, literal father has been continuously criticized for its racist use. Lacan, on the other hand, always returns us to Woman. For Lacan, She is the symptom of Man, the repressed truth that he too is lack-in-having. What this means in the context of feminism is that it returns us to the re-symbolization of the maternal function and of the feminine within sexual difference. More generally, we may use this insight as a locus for change, rather than emphasizing the participation of men in child raising. Of course, Lacan would deny that such a re-symbolization of the maternal function or of the feminine within sexual difference is possible. On my reading, as we will see, it is precisely because there is no established signified for Woman in the symbolic order that makes it impossible for the meaning of Woman to be stabilized so as to foreclose this process of re-symbolization.

On a broader scale, challenges to the dearth of symbolization of the feminine imply a critique of our notions of civilized order, an order profoundly influenced by our unconscious acceptance of the structures of gender. This is why I argue that the liberation of women implies a concept of liberation that would have implications for us all. Thus, this brand of feminism is not just about women and is not just one more special interest. It is about re-thinking the very basis for civilization and the re-imagining of a form of life in which we all might be significantly less discontented.

Let me turn now to how Lacan allows us to develop an explanation of why feminism is so difficult to maintain as a movement and how and why this difficulty is associated with the dearth of symbolizations for the feminine within sexual difference. We need to look more specifically at Lacan's analysis of why there can be no fixed signified for Woman within the symbolic order. In Lacan, we enter our culture and our unique status as speaking beings on the basis of our radical cut from the maternal body. This "scar of the navel" is not only actual in birth, it is also a symbolic tear that rips us away from the imaginary mother/child dyad.[49] The introduction of the child into the symbolic order is at the expense of his Mother/Other and all that she represents: a fantasy world of fulfilled desire. The law that imposes this symbolic castration is the law of the imaginary father whose potency is symbolized in the actual institutional structures and laws of patriarchal culture. The signifier for this potency is the phallus, which we know only in its expression as the law that bars us from the Mother. This explains why for Lacan the ultimate cultural law is the law imposed by the Oedipus complex. Both sexes are barred by the law imposed by the Name of the Father and all that it comes to represent in patriarchal culture. By patriarchal culture I mean a social order that organizes our sexual relations through patrilineal lineage. But the unconscious identification between the penis and the phallus positions the two sexes in different fields of significance for the assumption of gender identity. Thus, the bar to symbolization of the desire of the Mother has different implications for those of us who will be designated as masculine or feminine.

The little boy can identify himself with masculine culture through his projection of his likeness to the father who has the penis. It is this unconscious identification of the phallus with the penis that allows the little boy at least on the level of fantasy to compensate for the fundamental loss he has to endure. Psychically, those who become men have their subjectivity organized around this fantasy and accept the tolls of civilization precisely because of the compensation it offers for a primary loss, an imaginary world where discontentment would not be the price we pay for becoming human. The "bad news" for the little boy is that this fantasy leaves him in a constant state of anxiety before the terror that what makes him a man can always be taken away from him by the imaginary father with whom he unconsciously identifies. The endless substitutions for this father, in the form of deans, politicians and other figures of powerful men leave him in a state of unconsciously accepted subordination. His masculinity is always on the line and thus we have an explanation of the gesture mandated by the pecking order amongst men: "Just don't take it away from me and I'll work sixteen hours a day and never talk back." This is hardly an account of actual male superiority, yet it is an account of why men need the fantasy that they are superior to women. It is compensation for the toll of a primary loss. This loss generates the psychical fantasy of woman in which the lost Mother becomes a split imaginary figure, the infinitely desirable one, the bad girl who offers infinite pleasure, and the safe mother and wife, who serves as a non-threatening substitute for the Phallic mother. On this account of masculinity, however, there is clearly a basis for an alliance to challenge the structures of gender. The two sexes are divided into different fields of significance. Men are construed in relation to signifiers that are different from the ones to which women relate. The subjectivity of the masculine subject is guaranteed a fixed position in the realm reigned by phallic reference. But the price paid for this fixed position is still a form of symbolic castration. As a result, if the struggles of men against the structures of gender would never be the same as those of a woman, there is still a basis for a call to men to resist the imposition of traditional notions of masculinity.

Women, by contrast, because they are barred from the Mother and thus a primary signifier by which to organize their identity, cannot find "themselves" in the order of the symbolic. Women find only the split image of themselves imposed by the psychical fantasy of woman. Either we take on these images or we are left without representations of our "selves." If the privilege of the phallus as the primary signifier of sexual difference fixes man in his subject position, it dislocates woman from any fixed position on which to ground her subjectivity. What is left over, for Lacan, is beyond expression. The feminine imaginary cannot be given form because it cannot find the symbolic "stuff" to register the diversification of feminine sexual difference.

This Lacanian account explains why in popular terms women have trouble developing a positive "self-image." The images unconsciously associated with femininity are "bad" in the sense that they are inadequate in the richness of expression to adequately encompass any woman's life. For Lacan, the law of civilization is that we as women are denied access to a field of significance in which we could re-symbolize ourselves and have the "words to say" who we are. Thus, there can be no ground for identity for women. Women, paradoxically put, "are" without identity precisely because they are identified as lack. As the figure of the castrated Other, women can only signify what is not there. Barred in ourselves and from ourselves, we are the ultimate objects of desire. The hole we leave in reality is filled with masculine fantasy. As women we are only present through representations of the feminine Other, and these representations set the stage for a very limited conversation. Any theory of communication, particular of dialogic relationality, will have to confront how the feminine Other is seen. Who one sees as the interlocutor will influence the commitments in the conversation. Such representations will also limit the possibilities of articulation of who one is. Thus, a critical appropriation of Lacan helps us understand the relation between the dearth of symbolizations of the feminine within sexual difference and the experience of silencing which has often been attested to within the feminist movement. Not only do we need to listen to women's voices, we also need to know how and why the dearth of symbolizations puts a limit on our speech as we struggle to find the "words to say it."

For Lacan, our only alternative to our position as the feminine Other, man's trope for his own effort to tame the uncanny,[50] is to reposition ourselves on the side of the masculine, appropriate the phallus, and thus become lawyers, doctors, professors, etc. But then we will not be able to express our power as feminine. The repudiation of femininity, therefore, is inevitable if we are to be allowed entrance into the boys' club. For Lacan, feminism cannot represent itself as a feminism that includes the symbolization of the power of the feminine within sexual difference. Feminism will itself be barred as other than the appropriation of the phallic position and feminists will in turn be split by the psychical fantasy of woman. Here we have a cultural explanation of the phenomenon of critiques of feminism that themselves re-inscribe the limited symbolizations of feminine sexual difference. The "sexy" young woman is pitted against the figure she represents as the feminist, the older asexual woman who mistakenly politicizes her own unhappiness.[51] Sexuality is presented as tamed in that it identifies "sex" within the parameters set by a masculine symbolic. To have sex we have to play the game, but it is not such a terrible game even if it includes date rape because we get to have "sex." But what kind of "sex" is it that we get to have? We get to remain the desirable feminine other against those unattractive older spinsters who are not having sex. On the other hand, we are told to represent ourselves as if we had the qualities associated with the phallus, such as powerful women in the board room who "fuck back" and sell stock at the same time.[52] Lacan helps us to understand why recent books that focus on how feminists should re-represent themselves are no coincidence and, more importantly, why they inevitably replicate the limited representative options of our "sex."[53] Although this recent battle has taken place in the field of representation, it has not challenged the parameters of the field. But can we challenge those parameters? Lacanian analysis helps us explore the bar that feminism runs up against and therefore helps us to think differently about what we are fighting. But it also leaves us with no escape. We are locked into the masculine symbolic, fated to bang our heads against the wall.

IV. The Significance of Different Conceptions of the Limit

This conception of fate in Lacan, of the way in which the law of gender is reinforced by the bar as the phallus, demands a transcendental semantics. It is this transcendental semantics that secures the meaning of gender as it bars other possibilities. In transcendental semantics meaning is bounded only at the expense of blocking the sliding of signifiers, including in Lacan's case, the signifiers of the masculine and feminine and the signifieds they have come to articulate. Lacan's conception of the limit of meaning then yields to Derrida's deconstruction of Husserl's distinction between *Sinn* and *Bedeutung* or the sense, or meaning, of a word and its reference. For reasons of space I cannot repeat in detail how Derrida uses his deconstruction of Husserl's distinction between *Sinn* and *Bedeutung* against Lacan's philosophical claim that the phallus operates as a bar to the sliding of the signifier of the feminine.[54] Let me stress, however, that different conceptions of the limit are important for feminism.

By definition, a transcendental signifier must be true to its form. But since we cannot know it directly, but only in its expression and representations, it cannot achieve that purity. The very project of purifying the concept of form gets bogged down by the productivity of language in which it must be manifested and explained. It would only be possible to achieve the goal of transcendental semantics if expression and representation did nothing more than transport a constituted sense of the exterior, and by so doing, reissue a *noematic* sense, by providing access to conceptual form. The phallus can only be maintained in the position of the transcendental signifier if it can escape the ellipsis inevitably associated with linguistic expression and representation. But could it and it alone be uniquely salvaged from the fate of the transcendental signifier? As Derrida shows us, the "presence" of the same signifier, the phallus, as the signifier of all signifiers depends on the establishment of the *point de capiton*—the "quilting point" which for Lacan binds the subject to discourse—and thereby constitutes both as such —so that there will be one trajectory of repression that will lead us back to the phallus.[55] And it is only the phallus that can guarantee the trajectory of repression. As a result, Lacan cannot deduce the status of the phallus from the trajectory of repression established by the foreclosure in the symbolic order of feminine sexual difference. Without the prior establishment of the phallus in the position of the transcendental signifier there would be other possible trajectories. In the place of a transcendental deduction there is a circular argument which cannot maintain the phallus in its transcendental place and thus, Woman in her place as the castrated Other.

If it is, moreover, crucial for the masculinization of the phallus that it be unconsciously identified with the penis. For Lacan, no "body" has the phallus because as the bar that signifies the lack in both sexes it does not and cannot have a positive existence. This is why he must give the phallus a transcendental place if he is to bound the signifiers masculine and feminine absolutely. But the unconscious registration that Lacan also notes as inevitable—that no "body" has the phallus—means that the penis can be relocated from this identificatory structure and that other possibilities besides Woman can stand in for the figure of castration. These possibilities would mean that the signifier Woman and the field of significance in which she was positioned could not be philosophically bounded. The parameters and the limits of Her meaning always remain open to the possibility that they will be challenged. It is precisely the purpose of Derrida's deconstruction to show us that there can be no such binding of the signifier of the feminine.

The figure of the barred Woman, of Woman herself as the representation of the limit to meaning, is a figure fixed before the eyes through the congelation of meaning. The Woman allegorized as excess is one more fixture of her position, itself compelled by the law that forecloses the refiguration of the feminine within sexual difference. As an expression of the law of the phallus that he deconstructs, Derrida illustrates the ambivalent value of this allegorized figure. The figure as the representation of what cannot be represented expresses both the disruptive power of what remains uncanny and, as a condensation into a figure, the taming of the uncanny. The condensation of the figure points beyond to the metonymy of the signifier Woman which has no fixed signified. This ambivalent value includes for feminism the figure of the Woman outside the system who slides out from under its strictures and dictates.[56] If women's liberation is represented as the struggle for inclusion into the system of phallogocentric culture, then this figure represents a radical alternative. It is this radical alternative that fascinates Derrida.[57]

Derrida does not deny the congelation of meaning through the deeply inscribed codes of repetition that reinforce the gender hierarchy. His deconstruction is of Lacan's philosophical claim that these codes of repetition will be shielded from the iterability of their meaning. The bar itself cannot be conceptualized as an absolute limit. We can only know the bar as a metaphor, and like all metaphors the excess inherent in the identification through transference points beyond itself. Thus paradoxically, the limit recedes before its linguistic expression.

This is the paradox that Wittgenstein tirelessly returns us to in his philosophical investigations. His philosophical conclusion was that a form of life or a language game could never be known as a self-identical form. But there was an even greater paradox for Wittgenstein: It is through the very attempt to conceptualize the limit that we run up first against the limit of philosophical justification and then of sense itself. We run up against the limit precisely as it recedes before our attempts to adequately conceptualize it. But how can one run up against that which recedes when we try to describe it? How can the limit be there when it cannot be known? Wittgenstein knew that he could not use traditional philosophical explanation to illustrate this paradox. Yet it was precisely this irresolvable paradox which was the limit for Wittgenstein of philosophical justification. His highly original style which demonstrated the inevitability of running into this paradox was adopted because it was the only style adequate to the task of evoking the limit of language that both operates to give us a form of life and a world of sense and yet recedes before our attempt to conceptualize it. Perhaps Ursula K. Le Guin's allegory of the wall as boundary in the opening lines of *The Dispossessed* can help to give metaphoric expression to the limit understood as a paradox.

> There was a wall but it did not look unimportant. It was made of uncut rocks and roughly mortared. An adult could look right over it, and even a child could climb it. Where it crossed the roadway, instead of having a gate it degenerated into mere geometry, a line, an idea of a boundary. But the idea was real. It was important. For seven generations there had been nothing in the world more important than that wall. Like all walls it was ambiguous, two-faced. What was inside and what was outside it depended on which side of it you were on.[58]

And why use an allegory? Why not just say it directly? The answer is that the limit can only be evoked precisely because it eludes direct expression. Thus, the use of metaphor, of allegory, is not utilized as part of academic chic. Such devices are used to be faithful to the truth of paradox, to show what cannot be stated. What I have just said of Wittgenstein's style can also be said of the style of Derrida.

But there is an ethical moment in the endless demonstration of this paradox. It is the significance of this ethical moment that is particularly crucial for feminism. The demonstration of the limit of meaning loosens the binds of convention. The knots are loosened rather than re-enforced by philosophy. This challenge to any attempt to philosophically secure the bounds of meaning implicitly defends the possibility that we operate within an ever wider field of meaning. As the boundary recedes, we have more space to dream and re-imagine our forms of life. The very impossibility of knowing the boundaries that guarantee meaning is unsettling if one seeks security in an established world of sense. But as feminists know only too well, we have been tied down by the bounds of the meaning of femininity. The very impossibility of knowing the limit opens an endless horizon. As feminists, then, we have every reason to push against and beyond the boundaries.

As I have already noted, the recession of the boundary does not mean that the limit is not "there." Feminism operates from both sides of the paradox. Limit metaphors abound in feminism precisely because of the barriers, both external and those we have internalized, to expanding the range of meanings that have been given to the feminine within sexual difference. Even if Lacan's philosophical claim for the status of the phallus does not hold up against Derrida's deconstruction, his insight that the phallus is the privileged signifier in the unconscious for creativity and reproductive power remains important as an account of the barrier to the re-symbolization of the feminine within sexual difference. The attraction of Lacan to feminists is that he offers us a powerful cultural narrative of why the struggle to expand the symbolizations of the feminine within sexual difference has been so difficult. In a sense, we use Lacan to work backward and to move downward. We move from our conscious experience to an articulation of what must be the underlying conditions of our experience. This movement is obviously not a transcendental deduction in any strong sense. But in a weak sense we can use this deductive process to help us illuminate the conditions of our experience so that we can better understand what we are up against. We can use this understanding in the struggle to loosen the bounds of the imposed and rigid meanings given to the masculine and the feminine.

Thus, psychoanalysis gives us another dimension to the limit, a dimension that we can label the unconscious. Although Wittgenstein himself was suspicious of psychoanalysis, the unconscious, understood as a kind of unity, yields to the Wittgensteinian reading of the limit as paradox outlined earlier. For Lacan, the unconscious is continually generated as the isolation of usually imagistic signifiers and their corresponding relegation to the position of the signified. The unconscious, in other words, "is not"; it is rather always coming to be. Repression explains the congealing of the process and allows us to explain why certain signifiers have become so frozen into their status as signified they no longer seem to be governed by principles of metonymy and metaphor. Indeed, the emphasis in Lacan and what has come to be known as Lacanian feminism on the linguistic generation of the unconscious can itself be understood as an attempt to shed new light on why the limit of language in language can never be known. We can also add here that the bar between consciousness and the unconscious is not an absolute, but itself a function of language. An elaboration of metonymy and metaphor as principles of language help us understand both the congelation of meaning through repression and the unfreezing of these congealed meanings through the process of analysis. An understanding of the role of metonymy and metaphor can help us work from both sides of the paradox of the limit of meaning.

V. Feminism, Representation and the Enactment of Mimetic Identifications

The emphasis on metonymy and metaphor allows us to account for why the field of significance is expanding endlessly in its very articulation. Women writers consciously rely on the slippage of meaning inherent in a field of significance generated by metonymy and metaphor to elucidate new possibilities for the elaboration of experience. The emphasis then on these two principles of language is not only of theoretical import but of practical significance to the project of re-signifying the feminine within sexual difference.

But there is no neat way to separate the field of significance from the spheres of the imagination and of representation.[59] Lacan has helped us to understand why this is particularly the case when it comes to Woman. The very symbolic constructions of Woman are bound up with the fantasy projections unconsciously associated with the psychical fantasy of Woman. The struggle to give form brings us up against the limit of our imaginations. Evelyn Hammonds has argued eloquently that the suffering of African American women with AIDS has been obscured by the limits imposed both by racism and the psychical fantasy of Woman. They are viewed by the white male medical establishment as women of excess, as sexually irresponsible and drug abusers. They are blamed for their own suffering and thus, their own experience drops from sight. In like manner, they are ruthlessly "exposed" by the medical establishment's own stereotypes as to the cause of the disease amongst black women. Hammond, in her plea for visibility as crucial to the struggle against AIDS, further argues that the stereotypes of black women prevent them from being attractive media candidates. Their actual suffering fades from the scene. The message of the media is that AIDS is terrible because it kills artistic geniuses, not black women. Hammond eloquently draws these connections between limitations of the field of representation and political struggle of African American women AIDS victims. Hammond argues that the challenge of the representation of these women is crucial to giving them back their voice and for changing the terms of the struggle.

The enactment of mimetic identifications is a rhetorical and artistic device for both the engagement with and the displacement of the boundaries that have limited our imagination. I use the word enactment to indicate the conscious, politically committed engagement with the imagistic signifiers in relation to which we are construed as women. This enactment is explicitly mimetic in that it mimes. Miming not only implies mirroring but as enactment it is also a parody of what it mirrors. Miming *always* carries within it a moment of parody of what it mirrors. Such enactments are identifications in a dual sense. We can never know the levels to which we have internalized and identified ourselves with the available images of Woman. Unconscious identifications operate at such a deep level that we cannot separate ourselves from them. But when we enact an identification of one of the positions imposed upon by the fantasies and images of femininity we also stage the production of that image and that fantasy. By doing so, we create a distance from it and expose the gap between the fantasy and the complexity of actual women. Paradoxically, an enactment of a mimetic identification stages an identification so as to resist the stereotype associated with the image. The very lack of a fixed signified for Woman means that this sliding between the positionings of femininity is always possible.

The process of resymbolization takes place in the "in between" of the images and our lives. As feminists, we can enact the performative contradiction inherent in Lacan's analysis that Woman can have no fixed place in the masculine symbolic. Lacan interprets his analysis to mean that feminism is impossible because it must rest on a ground for Woman. But it is precisely because there is no firm ground for the identity of Woman that allows us to endlessly challenge any interpretation of us as our ultimate truth. As the meaning of woman is challenged as a limited set of fantasy constructions imposed upon rich and complex lives, as we widen the gap between ourselves and our representations and by so doing give birth to new modes of expression of feminine sexual difference, we also inevitably challenge the boundaries that have set masculinity and the parameters of normalized heterosexuality. We destabilize the foundations of man if we create further disruptions in the setting of ourselves as women. There can be no end to this process that finally gives us the truth of Woman.

Notes

1. I want to stress that what I have just written in no way denies the importance of social-scientific investigation. But it does demand that such investigations conduct themselves with careful attention as to how the symbolic constructions of what we know as femininity are "colored." For example, M. Patricia Fernandez Kelly has argued that certain policy recommendations that are purportedly based on the fact of the high rate of teenage pregnancy among African American women misunderstand the phenomenon they claim to know. In her subtle study, Kelly argues that the problem cannot be solved by making birth-control pills readily available to teenage African American women. She shows that implicit in many of the studies that such recommendations are based on is the assumption of the truth of the stereotype of the licentious "black" woman. The unconscious assumption that because "black" women are wild, you cannot control their sexuality but only try to control the consequences, is not only a racist stereotype, it prevents sound and wise policy recommendations from being made. On the other hand, Kelly offers an original analysis of what I would call the psychic motivation of African American teenagers that challenges the truth of the imagined wild "black"

woman. Kelly argues that due to race and class disadvantage which deny market opportunities and possibilities of individual achievement, African American women turn to sexuality and maternity as crucial markers in the ritualistic transition to adulthood. If we fail to understand the ritual, we will fail to adequately address the problem of teenage pregnancy, finding ourselves accomplices of the perpetuation of racial and sexual stereotypes as well. See "Rethinking Citizenship in the Global Village: Immigrants and the Underclass," a paper presented at "Figuring Feminism at the Fin de Siecle," Scripps College, 1993, on file with the author.

In her essay on African American women and AIDS, Evelyn M. Hammonds demonstrates how the suffering of women with AIDS has in part been erased by the imagined licentiousness and irresponsibility of African American women. The solution as with the teenage girls is "social hygiene." Hammonds argues that the fantasy of sexual degeneracy has a long history in the public, medical discourse on the sexuality of African American women. Hammonds further argues that because "black" women are in a very profound sense not imagined as "presentable" they have been both unconsciously and semi-consciously rejected as media symbols for the suffering of AIDS victims. See "Invisibility/Exposure: Black Women, Black Feminism and AIDS," also presented at "Figuring Feminism at the Fin de Siecle," Scripps College, 1993, on file with the author. In each of these cases, if the investigator fails to grapple with the way in which fantasies of the "black" woman informs what is taken for reality, he or she will confuse the projections of his or her own imagination with the so-called real world.

2. It is important to note that I by no means reject the importance of the elaboration of principles of justice. My only disagreement would be that such principles could never be philosophically justified in the strong Kantian sense of justification. Thus, I do disagree that there is one universalistic conception of the Right such as the one Jürgen Habermas attempts to locate in the pragmatic universals of communication. There is the specifically feminist criticism of any pure theory of Right: that it cannot address issues of sexuality such as pornography and sexual harassment as matters of right because these issues are "substantive." The two most renowned principles of justice with analytical jurisprudence are the liberty principle and the difference principle, elaborated and defended by John Rawls in his *Theory of Justice*. See John Rawls, *A Theory of Justice* (Cambridge: The Belknap Press, 1971). There is also a difficulty in expanding Rawls's principles to the issues of sexuality I just mentioned, including also the right to abortion. This difficulty inheres in the priority of the liberty principle and the conception of liberty Rawls accepts. These issues would have to

be addressed as questions of liberty and not of economic inequality. Thus, even the best feminist attempt to stretch Rawls's theory to address questions of gender has been misguided in its attempt to proceed through an analysis of the implication of the difference principle for questions of gender. See, for example, Susan Okin, *Justice, Gender, and the Family* (New York: Basic Books, 1989). But there is greater flexibility in Rawls's overall conceptualization of justice than in a proceduralist theory because of his emphasis on self-respect and the deleterious effects on a person's well-being of socially imposed shame. The shame expressed in being forced to keep one's sexuality in the closet would be a classic example of imposed sexual shame. Thus, we would need to use the concern with shame and self-respect to expand the principle of liberty to include what I have called minimum conditions of individuation. To expand Rawls's theory of justice in this manner is undoubtedly awkward, although I argue that it can be done. See Drucilla Cornell, *The Imaginary Domain*, (forthcoming, Routledge, 1995).

The reason for this awkwardness is that Rawls's theory of justice was developed to address questions of class and not of sex. Thus, I argue that we need to have a theory of justice particularly tailored to "sex." The need to expand even the most elegantly defended theory of justice shows the limits to a strong universalistic conception of the Right if such theories claim to be the last word on what constitutes the Right. But at least when Rawls has defended his theory of justice on the basis of reflexive equilibrium he has not made the claim that he offers a theory of the Right in the strong Kantian sense. See John Rawls, "The Domain of the Political Overlapping Consensus," New York University Law Review, vol. 64, no. 2 (1989), p. 233. Thus, it is philosophically consistent with his defense of his theory on the basis of reflexive equilibrium to argue that we need to develop a more expansive frame of justice to adequately address questions of sexuality as a matter of right. The very need for this addition shows the practical importance of always keeping what can constitute right, and the conception of the person on which rights are based open, so that we can contest and expand available rights.

3. I put the word "civilized" in quotation marks to draw attention to the way in which definitions of civilization come loaded with cultural prejudices. A classic example of how our prejudices are smuggled into our definitions of civilization can be founded in Sigmund Freud's struggle to clarify what "we" mean by civilization:

> We require civilized man to reverence beauty whenever he sees it in nature and to create it in the objects of his handiwork whenever he sees it in nature and to create it in the

objects of his handiwork in so far as he is able. But this is far from exhausting our demands on civilization. We expect besides to see the signs of cleanliness and order. We do not think highly on the cultural level of an English country town in Shakespeare's time when we read that there was a dung heap in front of his father's house in Stratford; we are indignant and call it "barbarous" (which is the opposite of civilized) when we find paths in the Wiener Wald littered with paper. Dirtiness of any kind seems to us incompatible with civilization.

See Sigmund Freud, *Civilization and Its Discontents*, trans. James Strachey (New York: W. W. Norton and Company, 1989).

4. See generally, Ludwig Wittgenstein, *Philosophical Investigations*, trans. G.E.M Anscombe (Oxford: Basil Blackwell, 1968).

5. I criticize Stanley Fish for making this error in his reading of Wittgenstein. (See "Convention and Critique," in *Transformations* (New York: Routledge, 1993)). Wittgenstein should also not be interpreted in any simple sense as a relativist, if relativism is understood to imply that we can consciously know the world as just there for us. When we see a green ball, we can only with great effort (if we can do it at all) see it as anything else but a green ball. The agreement in form of life is constitutive of objective reality. Thus, Wittgenstein is not a conventionalist or a relativist, at least as these terms have traditionally been defined, but rather a challenger to the realist/conventionalist divide. Philosophically speaking, there is no reason why we cannot re-imagine our form of life, but it is obviously extremely difficult to do so. Consider how difficult it is "for us" to even imagine creates who are not "sexed" within constraints of gender identity. On the other hand, in her extraordinary novel *The Left Hand of Darkness*, Ursula K. Le Guin engages in exactly that imaginative effort and tells us a story of humans who are not "sexed" within the dichotomy of man and woman. And yet the earthling, at least in the beginning of his sojourn, cannot help seeing these humans "sexed" differently because their form of life does not know gender as either man or woman. Le Guin beautifully describes the struggle to engage another form of life so as to see the world of "sexed beings" differently:

> Though I had been nearly two years on Winter, I was still far from being able to see the people of the planet through their own eyes. I tried to but my efforts took the form of self-consciously seeing a Gethenian first as a man, then as

a woman, forcing him into those categories so irrelevant to his nature and so essential to my own. Thus as I sipped my smoking sour beer I thought that at table Estraven's performance had been womanly, all charm and tact and lack of substance, specious and adroit. Was it in fact this soft supple femininity that I disliked and distrusted in him? For it was impossible to think of him as a woman, that dark ironic presence near me in the firelight darkness, and yet whenever I thought of him as a man I felt a sense of falseness, of imposture: in him, or in my own attitude towards him? His voice was soft and rather resonant but not so deep, scarcely a man's voice, but scarcely a woman's voice either . . . but was it seeing?

Ursula K. Le Guin, *The Left Hand of Darkness* (New York: Ace Books, 1969), p. 12.

6. See generally, Jacques Derrida, "Le Facteur de la Verité" in *The Post Card: From Socrates to Freud and Beyond*, trans. Alan Bass (Chicago: University of Chicago Press, 1982).

7. See Drucilla Cornell, "What Is Post-Modernity, Anyway?", *The Philosophy of the Limit* (New York: Routledge, 1992).

8. See Drucilla Cornell, "The Ethical Significance of the Chiffonnier", in *The Philosophy of the Limit*, pp. 62–90.

9. See Jacques Derrida, "Plato's Pharmakon," in *Dissemination*, trans. Barbara Johnson (Chicago: University of Chicago Press, 1981).

10. For Freud, the dictates of gender identity in the form of laws regulating sexual behavior and more generally, the conduct of "men" in their social relationships, is crucial to the maintenance of civilization:

The last, but certainly not the least important, of the characteristic features of civilization remains to be assessed: the manner in which relationship of men to one another, their social relationships are regulated relationships which affect a person as a neighbor, as a source of help, as another person's sexual object, as a member of the family and of a State. Here it is especially difficult to keep clear of particular ideal demands and to see what is civilized in general. Perhaps we may begin by explaining that the element of civilization enters on the scene with the first attempt to regulate these relationships.

Sigmund Freud, *Civilization and Its Discontents*, trans. James Strachey (New York: W. W. Norton and Company, 1989), p. 48.

11. See Drucilla Cornell, "Feminine Writing, Metaphor, and Myth," *Beyond Accommodation* (New York: Routledge, 1991).

12. For example, Evelyn Hammonds has argued that the fading of African American women with AIDS involves their representation through a fantasy grid of the irresponsible, wild "black" woman that allows their suffering to drop from sight. A crucial part of the struggle then is to challenge this representation as fantasy and to displace it by re-envisioning the reality endured by African American women with AIDS. See "Invisibility and Exposure: Black Women, Black Feminism, and AIDS," a paper presented at Scripps College, November, 1993.

13. I borrow the phrase "psychical fantasy of Woman" from Jacques Lacan. See *Feminine Sexuality: Jacques Lacan and the Ecole Freudienne*, eds. Juliet Mitchell and Jacqueline Rose, trans. Jacqueline Rose (New York: W. W. Norton and Company, 1985). For a discussion of the operation of the psychical fantasy of Woman, see Introduction II in the same volume.

14. Two recent movies which testify to the hold on the imagination of this splitting of Woman into two kinds are *Fatal Attraction* and *Basic Instinct*.

15. I am borrowing the phrase from the title of the autobiographical novel, *Words To Say It*, by Marie Cardinal. See Marie Cardinal, *Words To Say It*, trans. Pat Goodheart (France: Van Vactor and Goodheart, 1984).

16. Cardinal's novel articulates how her inability to elaborate her rebellion against restrictive definitions of femininity led her body to express them for her in the form of betrayal by her own feminine body, interminable menstrual periods.

17. My elaboration of the significance of my understanding of the ethical relationship is an important point of connection between my three books, *Beyond Accommodation*, *The Philosophy of The Limit*, and *Transformations* (New York: Routledge, 1993).

18. I am deliberately using a broad brush in defining the ethical relationship. I am thus defining it more broadly than Emmanuel Lévinas with whom the phrase is usually associated. See generally, Emmanuel Lévinas, *Totality and Infinity: An Essay On Exteriority*, trans. Alphonso Lingis (Pittsburgh: Duquesne University Press, 1969).

19. Niklas Luhmann, "Paradigm Lost: On The Ethical Reflection Of Morality," *Thesis Eleven,* No, 29, p. 84.

20. See Charles Peirce, *The Collected Papers of Charles Sanders Peirce,* Vol. I and II, eds. Charles Hartshorne and Paul Weiss (Cambridge: The Belknap Press of the Harvard University Press, 1960).

21. Luhmann, "Paradigm Lost," p. 86.

22. See Roger Berkowitz, "A Judge's Tragic Hero: An Arendtian Critique of Judging," in Berkeley Graduate Review, Vol. I, 1994.

23. See Nietzsche, *The Genealogy of Morals* (New York: Gordon Press, 1974).

24. See John Rawls, *A Theory of Justice* (Cambridge, Mass.: Harvard University Press, 1971), pp. 136–142.

25. See Cornell, *Imaginary Domain.*

26. *Ibid.*

27. Forthcoming from Habermas.

28. See Rawls, *A Theory of Justice.*

29. See, generally, John Rawls, *Political Liberalism* (New York: Columbia University Press, 1993).

30. Cornell, *Imaginary Domain.*

31. See Drucilla Cornell, "Recollective Imagination and Legal Interpretation" in *Transformations* (New York: Routledge, 1993).

32. See Catharine MacKinnon, *Feminism Unmodified: Discourses on Life and Law* (Cambridge: Harvard University Press, 1987).

33. See Catharine MacKinnon, *Toward a Feminist Theory of the State* (Cambridge: Harvard University Press, 1989).

34. See my discussion of the tension within MacKinnon's view of consciousness raising in *Beyond Accommodation* (New York: Routledge, 1991), pp. 147–152.

35. Judith Butler, "Introduction," *Bodies That Matter* (New York: Routledge, 1993).

36. See generally, bell hooks, *Black Looks: Race and Representation* (Boston: South End Press, 1992 by Gloria Watkins).

37. See Simone de Beauvoir, *The Second Sex*, trans. H. M. Parshley (New York: Random House, 1974; Paris: Alfred A. Knopf, Inc. 1952).

38. See Simone de Beauvoir, *Letters to Sartre*, ed. and trans. Quentin Hoare (New York: Arcade Publishers, Inc., 1993).

39. A classic illustration of this illusion of escape is the fact that it is made possible only by another woman assuming our "feminine" responsibilities in child care. If there was ever a scene in which class and race privilege are played out on a daily basis, it is the scene of privatized child care.

40. See my "probing" of the metaphors of femininity that Emmanuel Lévinas uses in his attempt to evoke the ethical relation in "The Ethical, Political, and Juridical Significance of the End of Man," *The Philosophy of the Limit* (New York: Routledge, 1992).

41. See Jacques Derrida, "The Force of Law: The Mystical Foundation of Authority," *Cardozo Law Review,* Vol. 11, nos. 5–6 (1990).

42. See generally, Cornell, *Beyond Accommodation.*

43. See Jane Flax, *Thinking Fragments: Psychoanalysis, Feminism, and Postmodernism in the Contemporary West* (Berkeley: University of California Press, Ltd., 1990).

44. See, generally, Cornell, *Beyond Accommodation.*

45. Lacan, *Feminine Sexuality.*

46. See "Ain't I a Woman," a speech by Sojourner Truth. I share Gananath Obeyesekere's understanding of the phrase "work of culture." See generally Gananath Obeyesekere, *The Work of Culture* (Chicago: University of Chicago Press, 1990).

47. Please see Denise Riley, *Am I that Name? Feminism and the Category of "Woman" in History"* (New York: Macmillan, 1988).

48. See Eleanor Galenson and Herman Roiphe, "The Impact of Early Sexual Discovery on Mood, Defensive Organization and Symbolization," in *The Psychoanalytic Study of the Child,* vol. 26 (1972), p. 195.

49. I borrow the phrase "scar of the navel" from Elisabeth Bronfen. See "Femininity—Missing in Action," *Over Her Dead Body: Death, Femininity and the Aesthetic* (New York: Routledge, 1992), pp. 205–224.

50. See Shoshana Felman, "Rereading Femininity," *Yale French Studies,* no. 62, pp. 19–44, 1981.

51. See Katie Roiphe, *The Morning After: Sex, Fear and Feminism on Campus* (New York: Little, Brown and Company, 1993).

52. See Naomi Wolf, *Fire with Fire: The New Female Power and How It Will Change the 21st Century* (New York: Random House, 1993).

53. See Jacqueline Rose, *Sexuality in the Field of Vision* (London: Verso, 1986).

54. See Cornell, *Beyond Accommodation,* pp. 27–36.

55. See Jacques Derrida, "Le Facteur de la Vérité," *The Post Card.*

56. Thus, I disagree with Gayatri Spivak when she argues that Derrida uncritically endorses the figure of the Woman as the radical outsider. He instead works to show us the ambivalent value of this figure. The

ambivalent value is precisely that in her allegorization, her position is once again fixed. See Gayatri Chakravorty Spivak, "Feminism and Deconstruction Again: Negotiating With Unacknowledged Masculinism," *Between Feminism and Psychoanalysis*, ed. Teresa Brennan (London: Routledge, 1989).

57. See "Choreographies: An Interview with Christie V. MacDonald," *The Ear of the Other: Otobiography, Transference, Translation*, ed. C. MacDonald (Lincoln: University of Nebraska Press, 1989).

58. See Ursula K. Le Guin, *The Dispossessed* (New York: HarperCollins, 1974), p. 1.

59. See Teresa de Lauretis, *Alice Doesn't: Feminism, Semiotics, Cinema* (Bloomington, Indiana: Indiana University Press, 1984).

5

Subjectivity, Historiography, and Politics: Reflections on the "Feminism/Postmodernism Exchange"

Seyla Benhabib

Throughout the 1980s, and in fields as diverse as architectural theory, literary criticism, philosophy, and social theory, the term "postmodernism" was used to mark a diffuse sense of time-consciousness. This consciousness was defined by the widespread sentiment of the exhaustion of the project of modernity, of being at the end of certain cultural, theoretical, and social-political paradigms. As is often the case with terms attempting to capture the *Zeitgeist*, the very definition of these terms themselves become aspects of the *Zeitgeist*. It is often difficult to distinguish between the signifier and the signified; the former becomes implicated in the identity of the latter. So it was and continues to be with the term "postmodernism."

Judith Butler is impatient with this term. She is suspicious that the term is being used as a weapon of dismissal and delegitimation. She sees the term as homogenizing and lumping together to the point of unrecognizability divergent and often conflictual currents of thought. In particular, she implies that the term postmodernism is used to denigrate and to dismiss contemporary French philosophy. Butler's response reminds me of Foucault's quip: "What is postmodernism? I'm not up to date."[1]

This response, however, misses the spirit and purpose of my first contribution. Precisely because I did not want to use the occasion given to us by the Greater Philadelphia Philosophy Consortium in the Fall of 1990 to rehearse the *"dialogue des sourds,"* which has so far characterized exchanges between critical social theory and post-structuralist French philosophy, I situated the working definition of the postmodern moment for the purposes of this debate among us, as feminist theorists, with reference to Jane Flax's work. Flax has given us a clear and cogent characterization of some aspects of the diffuse *Zeitgeist* called postmodernism, and it is with reference to her theses that I initiated the discussion. Butler also misconstrues the spirit of my remarks in not taking at all seriously what was involved in the attempt to distinguish between "strong" and "weak" versions of the theses of the Death of the Subject, Death of History, and Death of Metaphysics. As I argued in my previous work on Jean-François Lyotard, while I see the term postmodern as being useful to mark a sense of time-consciousness in culture, philosophy, and social theory, my disagreement with Lyotard centers around the characterization of this "moment" and of the conceptual-political-philosophical options it allows. What I have called "the Demise of the Episteme of Representation" is in my view a more precise delineation of the transformations in the field of philosophy which constitute the postmodern condition.[2]

At the core of the disagreement between Butler and myself lie issues of subjectivity, selfhood, and agency. This should come as no surprise, insofar as questions of subjectivity and the challenge to our traditional understandings of selfhood and agency are crucial to the current juncture of philosophy and feminist theory. As Rosi Braidotti has recently written, "If feminist thought is clearly situated in the field of modernity, in the critique of the subject, it is because women's struggles are one of the facets of the same 'crisis,' and act as one of its deepest theoretical and political rhizomes or roots."[3] Judith Butler's views of the performative constitution of gender identity are among the most original and provocative writings by feminists on the crisis and question of subjectivity.

Wherein lies the disagreement? I doubt whether Butler's performative theory of the constitution of gender identity can do justice to the complexities of the ontogenetic origins of gender in the human person on the one hand, and whether, on the other hand, this view can anticipate, indicate, lead us to rethink a new configuration of subjectivity. In retrospect, I am ready to admit that my reading of *Gender Trouble* in the light of an Erving Goffmanesque theory of self-constitution may have been inadequate; by performativity Butler does not mean a theatrical but a speech-act model.[4] In an illuminating subsequent explication of this model she writes (in this volume): "To be constituted by language is to be produced within a given network of power/discourse which is open to resignification, redeployment, subversive citation from within and interruption and inadvertent convergence within such networks." What does it mean "to be constituted by language"? Are linguistic practices the *primary site* where we should be searching for an explication of gender constitution? What about other practices like family structures, child-rearing patterns, children's games, children's dress habits, schooling, cultural habitus etc? Not to mention of course the significance of the words, deeds, gestures, phantasies, and the bodily language of parents, and particularly of the mother in the constitution of the gender identity of the child. In *Gender Trouble* as well as in her "Postscript," I still see a tendency in Butler's work toward what Fraser has called the "privileging of linguistic metaphors."[5] At one level I completely agree with Butler that "the enabling conditions for an assertion of 'I' are provided by the structure of signification, the rules that regulate the legitimate and illegitimate invocation of that pronoun, the practices that establish the terms of intelligibility by which that pronoun can circulate."[6] The narrative codes of a culture define the content with which this pronoun "I" will be invested, the appropriate instances when it can be invoked, by whom and how.

Yet the historical and cultural study of diverse codes of the constitution of subjectivity, or the historical study of the formation of discursive practices of individuality, does not answer the question: what mechanisms and dynamics are involved in the developmental process through which the human infant, a vulnerable and dependent body, becomes a distinct self with the ability to speak its language and the ability to participate in the complex social processes which define its world? Such dynamics and mechanisms enabled the children of the ancient Egyptians to become members of that cultural community no less than they enabled Hopi children to become social individuals. The historical study of culturally diverse codes which define individuality cannot be equated with the study of those social processes through which a human infant becomes the social self, regardless of the cultural and normative content which defines selfhood in different socio-historical contexts. In the former case we are studying *structural processes* and *dynamics of socialization and individuation;* in the latter, historical and hermeneutic processes of signification and meaning-constitution.

In the concluding reflections to *Gender Trouble* Butler returns to questions of agency, identity and politics. She writes:

> The question of locating "agency" is usually associated with the viability of the "subject," where the subject is understood to have some stable existence prior to the cultural field that it negotiated. Or, if the subject is culturally constructed, it is nevertheless vested with an agency, usually figured as the capacity for reflexive mediation, that remains intact regardless of its cultural embeddedness. On such a model, "culture" and "discourse" *mire* the subject, but do not constitute that subject. This move to qualify and to enmire the preexisting subject has appeared necessary to establish a point of agency that is not fully *determined* by that culture and discourse. And yet, this kind of reasoning falsely presumes (a) agency can only be established through recourse to a prediscursive "I," even if that "I" is found in the midst of a discursive convergence, and (b) that to be *constituted* by discourse is to be *determined* by discourse, where determination forecloses the possibility of agency.[7]

Indeed the question is: how can one be constituted by discourse without being determined by it? A speech-act theory of performative gender constitution cannot give us a sufficiently thick and rich account of gender formation that would also explain the capacities of human agents for self-determination. What is it that enables the self to "vary" the gender codes such as to resist hegemonic discourses? What psychic, intellectual, or other sources of creativity and resistance must we attribute to human subjects for such variation to be possible?[8]

The theory of performativity, even if Butler would like to distinguish gender-constitution from identity-constitution, still presupposes a remarkably deterministic view of individuation and socialization processes which falls short of the currently available social-scientific reflections on the subject.[9] The viability of some form of human agency, however, is crucial to make empirical sense of processes of psycho-sexual development and maturation.[10] To embark upon a meaningful investigation of these issues from where we stand today would not involve yet another decoding of metaphors and tropes about the self, but a serious interchange between philosophy and other social sciences like socio-linguistics, social interactionist psychology, socialization theory, psychoanalysis, and cultural history, among others.

The dispute then between Butler and myself around issues of gender-constitution, the self and identity has two levels: First, what kind of empirical social research paradigms is Butler privileging in her views of gender constitution as performativity? Are these adequate for the explanation of ontogenetic processes of development? Second, what normative vision of agency follows from, or is implied by this theory of performativity? Can the theory account for the capacities of agency and resignification it wants to attribute to individuals, thus explaining not only the constitution of the self but also the resistance that this very self is capable of in the face of power/discourse regimes? Butler and I agree that to make sense of the struggles of women, to make sense of the struggles of gays and lesbians to change contemporary gender codes, as theorists, we must at least create the conceptual space for thinking of the possibility of agency, resignification, subversive deployment.

Whereas the disagreements between Butler, Cornell and myself are of an *interparadigmatic* nature, enframed by different traditions of philosophical thought, the differences between Nancy Fraser and myself are *intraparadigmatic* and involve matters of degree and nuance rather than a clash of theoretical paradigms. As Fraser argues, it may be that the antithesis between critical theory and post-structuralism is arid and unnecessary, and that we should go beyond it. Yet I disagree with her that it is "false." There are serious differences here and genuinely different conceptual options.

One of the bones of contention between Fraser and myself concerns her and Linda Nicholson's joint call for "postmodernist feminist theory," which would be pragmatic and fallibilistic, "that would tailor its method and categories to the specific task at hand, using multiple categories when appropriate and foreswearing the metaphysical comfort of a single feminist epistemology." (in this volume) In view of their preference for this research paradigm, Fraser takes me to task and complains, "Instead of staking out the middle position that her own argument requires, she concludes by doubting that feminist historiography can be postmodern in *any* sense and still retain an interest in emancipation (in this volume)." My response is that the even-handed and commonsensical approach to tailoring theory to the tasks at hand, advocated by Fraser and Nicholson, is not postmodern. Fraser can reconcile her political commitments with a theoretical sympathy to postmodernism, only because in effect she has replaced "postmodern" by "neo-pragmatist" historiography and social research. As opposed to the pragmatic pluralism of methodological approaches guided by research interests, as advocated by Fraser, what postmodernist historiography displays is an "aesthetic" proliferation of styles which increasingly blur the distinctions between history and literature, factual narrative and imaginary creation. In a general review article of postmodern trends in historiography, F. R. Ankersmit writes: ". . . because of the incommensurability of historiographical views—that is to say, the fact that the nature of historical differences of opinion cannot be satisfactorily defined in terms of research subjects—there remains nothing for us to do but to concentrate on the style embodied in every historical view or way of looking at the past, if we are to guarantee the meaningful progress of historical debate. Style, not content, is the issue in such debates. Content is derivative of style."[11]

A recent debate between two eminent feminist historians brought to light extremely well some of the conceptual and normative "antitheses" involved in the methodological construction of different historical paradigms. If we can abstract for a moment from the ultimately futile question of whether Michel Foucault is a postmodernist or not, and focus instead on the implications of his philosophy of discourse/power for social research and historiography, the debate between Linda Gordon and Joan Scott is extremely illuminating for clarifying some of the misgivings I have expressed about the "emancipatory" implications of certain narratological strategies.

The Summer 1990 issue of the journal *Signs* carried an exchange between Linda Gordon and Joan Scott which involved reviews by each of the other's recent books and the authors' responses.[12] Central to debates in contemporary feminist historiography no less than in philosophy and cultural analysis is the status of the subject and of subjectivity. After reviewing Linda Gordon's presentation of the history of family violence as it was treated and defined by professional social workers in three child-saving agencies in Boston from the 1880's to the 1960's, Scott observes that Gordon's book "is aimed at refuting simple theories of social control and rejecting interpretations that stress the top-down nature of welfare policies and the passivity of their recipients."[13] Instead Gordon proposes an interactive model of relationships, according to which power is negotiated among family members and among the victims and state agencies. Joan Scott sees little evidence for women as "active agents" in Gordon's book; the title of Gordon's book—*Heroes of Their Own Lives: The Politics and History of Family Violence*—Scott observes "is more a wish than a historical reality, more a politically correct formulation than anything that can be substantiated by the sources."[14] And the methodological difficulty is stated succinctly, in terms which immediately remind us of Butler's claims examined previously on the "social and cultural construction of agency." "A different conceptualization of agency," writes Scott, "might have avoided the contradictions Gordon runs into and articulated better the complex relationship between welfare workers and their clients evident in the book. *This conceptualization would see agency not as an attribute or trait inhering in the will of autonomous individual subjects, but as a discursive effect, in this case the effect of social workers' constructions of families, gender, and family violence. It would take the idea of 'construction' seriously, as something that has positive social effects. (For the most part Gordon uses 'construction' as if it were synonymous with 'definition,' but definition lacks the materiality connoted by 'construction.')* It was, after all, the existence of welfare societies that not only made family violence a problem to be dealt with but also gave family members a place to turn to, a sense of responsibility, a reason for acting, and a way of thinking about resistance" (emphases added).[15]

One sees in Scott's critique of Gordon's book a clash of paradigms within women's historiography[16]—a clash between the social history from below paradigm used by Gordon, the task of which is to illuminate the gender, class and race struggles through which power is negotiated, subverted, as well as resisted to by the so-called "victims" of history, and the paradigm of historiography, influenced by Foucault's work, in which the emphasis is on the "construction" of the agency of the victims through mechanisms of social and discursive control from the top. Just as for Michel Foucault there is no history of the victims but only a history of the construction of victimization, a history of the agencies of victim control, so too for Scott as well, it is the "social construction of family violence," rather than the actual lives of the victims of family violence which is methodologically central.[17] Just as for Foucault every act of resistance is but another manifestation of an omnipresent discourse-power complex, for Scott too, women who negotiate and resist power do not exist; the only struggles in history are between competing paradigms of discourses, power-knowledge complexes.[18]

Let me tread lightly here: not being a professional historian, I am in no position to arbitrate the dispute between Joan Scott and Linda Gordon as to its historical merits. Instead I am calling attention to some of the conceptual issues involved. We see, in Scott's critique of Gordon, how Foucauldian premises about the social "construction of agency" are juxtaposed to the history from below approach espoused by Gordon. If we go along with Joan Scott, one approach to feminist historiography follows; and another, if we are with Gordon. Of course, it could also be that there is no either/or here, that each method and approach should learn from and benefit from the other. Yet before we can issue a Polyanna call to all parties of the debate, we should clarify what the conceptual constraints of postmodernist historiography are for feminists and others. Linda Gordon, I think, puts the matter very succinctly: "In fact Scott's and my differences go to the heart of contemporary controversies about the meanings of gender. Scott's determinist perspective emphasizes gender as 'difference,' marked by the otherness and absolute silencing of women. I use gender to describe a power system in which women are subordinated through relations that are contradictory, ambiguous, and conflictual—a subordination maintained against resistance, in which women have by no means always defined themselves as other, in which women face and take choices and action despite constriction. These are only two of many versions of gender, and they are by no means opposite, but they may illuminate the relevant issues here."[19]

We see once more that these antitheses are not false but quite real: agreement alone on the end of historical metanarratives either of the Marxian, centered around class struggle, or of the liberal sort, centered around a notion of progress is no longer sufficient. Beyond such agreement begin difficult questions about the relationship of historiography, politics, and memory. Should we approach history to retrieve from it the victims' memories, lost struggles and unsuccessful resistances, or should we approach history to retrieve from it the monotonous succession of infinite "power/knowledge" complexes that constitute selves? As Linda Gordon points out, these methodological approaches also have implications for how we should think of "gender."

In an earlier essay, "Gender, Sex and Equivalent Rights,"[20] Drucilla Cornell took to task my criticism about the mystificatory locutions which seemed to follow from the method of deconstruction concerning gender identity. A more serious exchange on the virtues and limits of contemporary deconstructionist philosophy will have to await another occasion.[21] More generally, Cornell argues against my claim, also taken to task by Butler, that views of selfhood and agency which follow from certain contemporary French philosophies render incoherent, problematic, conceptually confused, women's own struggles for autonomy, agency, and equality. In an elegant and deft reworking of Lacanian psychoanalytic themes in conjunction with deconstructionist philosophy, Cornell has created a unique voice for herself in the intersection of feminist theory and critical legal studies. Yet it is the nature and coherence of this synthesis which I question.

When writing as a critical legal theorist, Cornell proceeds from an internal, immanent critique of the norms of American liberalism and jurisprudence. In her essay, "Gender, Sex, and Equivalent Rights," for example, she introduces a distinction between gender, sexuality, and sex, and then proceeds to criticize Justice White's majority opinion in *Bowers v. Hardwick* which reduced homosexuality to the performance of acts of sodomy. The distinction between sex (physiological, bodily characteristics), gender identity (the socio-cultural and psychic construction of a "female" and a "male" type supposedly corresponding to these differences), and lived sexuality (whether a woman with female physiological characteristics expresses herself sexually as a "female" in a relation to a man, or as a male or female in relation to another woman) is interesting and useful. Indeed it allows Cornell to pinpoint the absolute objectification of homeosexual identity implied by the Supreme Court's reduction of homosexuality to the performance of a specific type of bodily act—which of course heterosexual couples as well can perform.[22] But such a distinction can be drawn on the basis of any number of different psychoanalytic and philosophical traditions besides deconstruction. Most recent feminist psychoanalytic work in the USA, like the work of Nancy Chodorow and Jessica Benjamin, also operates with such distinctions.[23] To accept as complex and opaque an edifice as Lacanian psychoanalysis or Derridean deconstruction on these grounds alone will not do. I know that Cornell has elsewhere presented more extensive arguments on behalf of these traditions.[24]

Yet if the relationship between these conceptual frameworks and the critique of legal theory which Cornell undertakes is a contingent one, what does this suggest for the relation between political/legal normative claims and postmodernist philosophical positions? Does Cornell think that the task of expanding the female imaginary such as to reinscribe a utopian female sexuality can suffice for feminist theory and politics? Indeed, I am and continue to be skeptical about the place of the aesthetic in feminist politics, not because I dismiss the aesthetic, but because like Max Weber and Jürgen Habermas, I think that the logics of the realm of the aesthetic, the ethical, the juridical, and the political have been differentiated in modern societies. No theoretical or political gains are attained by blurring these boundaries; although in a vital culture and a flourishing social order they must continuously, critically, and contentiously interact.[25]

In her work as a critical legal theorist Cornell unavoidably deploys the political and legal vocabularies of liberal democracies for creating the institutional and discursive space within which to articulate the claims of oppressed social and sexual minorities. Listen to Cornell's language: relying on Amartya Sen's definition, she understands equivalent rights as equality of capability and well-being, where capability "reflects a *person's freedom* to choose between different ways of living" (Sen); "how can women's reproductive capacity . . . be *valued* and legally protected?"; "the very devalorization of the feminine and the definition of heterosexuality as 'normal' makes it difficult for women and homosexuals to participate in their community without the *shame* of their 'sex' or their sexuality"; "the division between normal, heterosexual and abnormal, homosexual 'sexual identity'— *as long as that identity is based on consent between adults*—is a cultural construction" (emphases added). This is the language of "old-fashioned" humanistic liberal-democratic theory: the call for the law to enhance the autonomy and individuality of selves rather than to silence and humiliate them; the assertion of the equal human worth and dignity of repressed minorities—gay men and lesbian women— and the call to end their being cast in "shame"; finally, the invocation of the criterion of "consensual sex betwen adults," thus eliminating enforced homosexuality, child molestation, and pederasty from categories of sexuality that we should protect. For me the persistence of these "universalist" moral/legal/political locutions is not a problem; only I do not see how or why Cornell thinks that a Lacanian or a Derridean project is either indispensable or necessary to enframe these claims, when, on the surface of it, neither Lacan nor Derrida endorses the language of democratic-liberal humanism.

As Cornell undoubtedly knows, "the aspiration to a nonviolent relationship to the Other and to otherness more generally" is one that we share, and which enters our work through the influence of Adorno's thought in my case, Levinas as well as Adorno in hers.[26] Only, I find this formulation inadequate for distinguishing between justice and the ethical. Justice requires not only nonviolence but also respect for the otherness of the other for whom I may feel no affection, in fact, for the one whose otherness may be repugnant to me. To resort to the earlier example in the *Bowers v. Hardwick* case: one of the reasons why this decision is unjust and reflects one of the worst moments of political opportunism in the history of the Supreme Court, when political convenience and the protection of state rights became the mask for disenfranchising a sexual minority, is the rampant disrespect shown by the majority opinion for the "otherness of the other." Justice White *et al.* need not have sympathy, empathy, or an ethical commitment to homosexual males whose lives they do not condone; but they have an obligation to respect their rights as citizens to be different and to practice this difference. The difficult legal and political questions begin at the point when we have to define the acceptable, fair, just limits of difference which a social order can or will want to live with. The injunction of the nonviolent relation to the Other is an ethical injunction which should permeate eveyday attitudes in institutions, as well as the media, in the culture at large as well as in our personal relations. Yet this injunction alone cannot serve as the basis of justice: quite to the contrary, it presupposes a universalistic justice insofar as it implies that every human person, no matter how different from us, must be treated as one to whom I owe respect. If we do not distinguish between this norm of universalistic justice and the ethical content of the injunction for a nonviolent relation to the other, we leave the identity of the other dangerously undefined. We run the risk of accepting definitions of otherness as ones to whom we owe a special obligation in virtue of our membership in this or that community. In order to prevent ethnocentric, religious, linguistic, sexual, racial, national definitions of otherness, in order to make sure that the norms of universal justice were fulfilled, I have sought to distinguish between the "generalized" and the "concrete" other.[27] Can the project of ethical feminism, which Cornell and I share, be based on the injunction to aspire to a non-violent relation to the Other alone? I do not think that this injunction is conceptually or politically rich and differentiated enough to serve as the foundation of social criticism.

By "normative foundations" of social criticism I mean exactly the conceptual possibility of justifying the norms of universal moral respect and egalitarian reciprocity on rational grounds; no more and no less. Whereas most of my colleagues in this volume seem to think that even this is in some sense too much, I think that to want to deny this point is like wanting to jump over our own shadow. The more controversial issue is not whether such normative justification is necessary, I do not know how we could do without it, but whether moral and political universalism is philosophically plausible without essentialism or transcendentalism of some sort or another. I have argued elsewhere for a "nonfoundationalist" justification of critical social theory and have expanded this strategy of justification in *Situating the Self*.[28]

Theoretically, we should be reluctant to cut the branch on which we sit, while using every opportunity and possibility to prune it and to make it blossom to reflect our differences as women; hence my call for reflection on foundations, which are of course, as Butler observes contingent, for the project of modernity itself is a contingent historical project. Politically, we should avoid two problematic alternatives: on the one hand, the placative use of certain norms and ideals to defend really existing capitalist democracies as if they were exempt from critique; on the other hand, the "*gauchiste*" illusion of thinking that one can struggle for the rights of the "permanent minorities of liberalism"[29] on any grounds other than the space created by the universalistic struggles of modernity since the American, French, Russian revolutions and various anti-imperialist struggles. We should not romanticize the "other" (as I am afraid Judith Butler does in her rather uncritical remarks about Saddam Hussein). Since the 16th and 17th centuries the project of modernity has been a global one; in this process there are no uniform, monolithic "others."[30] In every culture which was in some ways touched by the process of modernity, we find those who have fought for freedom, equality, and human dignity and those who have resisted such calls. Feminist theory is inevitably caught in the dialectic of modernity in which universalistic ideals first emerged, and within which they are continuously contested, evoked, challenged, and changed.

Notes

This response has been revised from the German original for inclusion in this volume. Notes 4, 5, 16, 20, 22, 25, and 26 have been added to the text, following our agreement that to avoid an infinite regress, we would respond to each others' responses around minor points only.

1. Gerard Raulet, "Structuralism and Post-Structuralism: An Interview with Michel Foucault," trans. Jeremy Harding, *Telos. A Quarterly Journal of Critical Thought* (Sping 1983), No. 55, pp. 195–211.

2. I am puzzled by Butler's statement in her footnote that "The conflation of Lyotard with the array of thinkers summarily positioned under the rubric of 'postmodernism' is performed by the title and essay by Seyla Benhabib, 'Epistemologies of Postmodernism: A Rejoinder to Jean-François Lyotard,' in *Feminism and Postmodernism,* ed. Linda Nicholson (New York: Routledge, 1989)." In some of his writings on aesthetic theory, Lyotard has insisted on characterizing his position as "high modernism," or as following the spirit of the modernist avant-garde. Lyotard's philosophical vision celebrates the end of grand narratives and of the irreconcilable plurality of discourses, language games, frameworks opened up by the end of such narratives of legitimation. The "agonistics of language" identified by Lyotard in *The Postmodern Condition* is not at all altered but only refined and situated with respect to the history of philosophy in his subsequent work *Le Différend*. See J.-F. Lyotard, *The Postmodern Condition,* trans. G. Bennington and Brian Massumi (Minneapolis: University of Minnesota Press, 1984), p. 10, and J.-F. Lyotard, *The Differend. Phrases in Dispute,* trans. Georges Van Den Abbeele (Minneapolis: University of Minnesota Press, 1988). The French edition appeared in 1983. I have dealt more extensively with the epistemology and politics of Lyotard's position in *Le Differend* in "Democracy and Difference. The Metapolitics of Lyotard and Derrida," *Journal of Political Philosophy,* Vol. 2, No. 1 (1994), pp. 1–23, and in "Demokratie und Differenz," in *Gemeinschaft und Gerechtigkeit,* ed. Micha Brumlik and Hauke Brunkhorst (Frankfurt: Fischer, 1993). Why does Butler assume that to disagree, even to disagree violently, as I do with Lyotard, is a form of careless dismissal of the thought of another? Is not disagreement a sign of respect for the significance of the position of the interlocutor?

3. Rosi Braidotti, *Patterns of Dissonance. A Study of Women in Contemporary Philosophy*, trans. Elizabeth Guild (London: Polity Press, 1991), p. 11.

4. It is true, as Judith Butler and Drucilla Cornell suggest in their respective responses, that this exchange also touches upon "the ethics of reading." I find the implication, however, that all disagreement implies a misreading or a misunderstanding to be a self-serving hypothesis. Sometimes misunderstandings may be willful and malicious and as such they have no redeeming value in intellectual debate; very often, though, misunderstandings arise among interlocutors because of unclarities in formulation, differences in theoretical traditions, styles of rhetorical expression, or creative misinterpretations. If, to use a felicitous phrase of Harold Bloom's, "all reading is a misreading," there may also be a creative moment, an unanticipated learning process, a process of illumination among interlocutors to a dialogue, which force one, entice or lead one to express better, more fruitfully what "one meant," but was misunderstood to have meant, etc. I continue to be of the opinion that the kinds of criticism of the "performative" theory of gender constitution which Fraser and I have raised against Butler were not instances of "careless" reading or willful "misreading," but that they went to the heart of certain unthought implications in her theory. The distinction, for example, between a theatrical and a linguistic concept of performativity was not sharply drawn in *Gender Trouble*. Particularly in those sections of *Gender Trouble* dealing with drag, cross-dressing, and the stylization of butch-femme identities (pp. 134 ff.), the theatrical and Goffmanesque metaphors of gender constitution, as opposed to the linguistic ones, become prominent.

5. There is an interesting tension, almost a fissure, in Butler's thinking on the subject of gender constitution. This is the fissure between psychoanalytic theory and Foucauldianism. In the section of *Gender Trouble* entitled "Prohibition, Psychoanalysis, and the Production of the Heterosexual Matrix," Butler discusses various psychoanalytic theories which see gender identity—homosexual as well as heterosexual—as a "melancholic structure," generated through a refusal of loss of the primary love object through its incorporation into the body (*Gender Trouble*, pp. 66 ff.). Repeatedly, however, the path opened by these psychoanalytic reflections on mourning and melancholia as they contribute to the formation of gender identity is closed off by the trope of the "discursive/linguistic critique," borrowed from Foucault. To quote Butler: "The effort to locate and describe a 'sexuality before the law' as a primary bisexuality or as an ideal and unconstrained

polymorphousness implies that the law is antecedent to sexuality ...
But if we apply the Foucauldian critique of the repressive hypothesis
to the incest taboo, that paradigmatic law of repression, then it would
appear that the law produces both sanctioned heterosexuality and
trasgressive homosexuality. Both are indeed *effects*, temporally and
ontogenetically later than the law itself, and the illusion of a sexuality
before the law is itself the creation of that law." (74) This
Foucauldian critique, which stresses that desire is an effect of the law
rather than preceding it, creates epistemological puzzles. The question
is, How do we know whether there is sexual desire with a marked
directionality which precedes "the law of culture" or whether all
human desire is essentially plastic and acquires its directionality by
being impacted upon by culture? The answer is that we do not, and
all theorizing about the "origins" of desire is a form of retrospective
speculation. Psychoanalysis is a retrospective theory which recon-
structs the sources of human suffering in the present through the past
history of the individual. There is no sexual ground-zero in this project of reconstruction; there is no stage either in individual analysis or
in theory which one could reach and postulate as being the point
where one can observe human desire in its "original form."
Psychoanalysis is interminable. In fact, the whole language of cause
and effect is inadequate here. Although we can only know about
human desire retrospectively, as refracted through the laws of language and individual memory, it does not follow that desire is purely
linguistic and disappears into language without residue. Psychoanalysis insists that there is recalcitrance at the core of human sexuality, which although epistemologically only accessible via the medium
of language, is not "linguistic" at its core. Whether that core is homosexual or heterosexual or polymorphous perverse is, I believe, irrelevant and may not even be knowable. The important point is that there
is a memory of the body and a materiality to the somatic dimension of
our linguistic existence for each individual. These cannot be reduced
to language and discursivity although being only epistemically accessible through language and other linguistically interpretable forms of
expression like bodily gestures, grimaces, symptoms, and phobias.
Judith Butler has pursued some of these questions, and particularly
objections to the radical constructivism of Foucault's framework, in
Bodies that Matter: On the Discursive Limits of Sex (New York:
Routledge, 1993).

Oddly enough, in wanting to "linguistify" the unconscious and
desire, the critical theory of Jürgen Habermas and the discourse theory of Foucault are not opposed to each other at all. See Joel
Whitebook, "Intersubjectivity and the Monadic Core of the Psyche:

Habermas and Castoriadis on the Unconscious," in *Praxis International*, vol. 9. No. 4 (January 1990), pp. 347–365; forthcoming in: Maurizio Passerin d'Entrèves and Seyla Benhabib, eds. *Habermas and the Unfinished Project of Modernity. Critical Essays on* The Philosophical Discourse of Modernity (Polity Press, 1994). See also Joel Whitebook, *Perversion and Utopia: A Study in Psychoanalysis and Critical Theory* (Forthcoming, MIT Press, 1995).

6. *Gender Trouble. Feminism and the Subversion of Identity* (New York: Routledge, 1990), p. 143.

7. *Gender Trouble*, p. 143. Emphasis in the text.

8. Alan Wolfe gives an illuminating account of what follows for social theory and normative thinking when concepts of selfhood are denied. In postmodernism as well as in systems-theoretic social science, Wolfe sees a "lack of appreciation for the rule-making, rule-applying, rule-interpreting capacities of human beings and an emphasis instead on the rule-following character. The price postmodernism pays for its flirtation with algorithmic conceptions of justice is a very high one: the denial of liberation, play, and spontaneity that inspired radical epistemologies in the first place." In: "Algorithmic Justice," *Cardozo Law Review*, special issue on "Deconstruction and the Possibility of Justice," Vol. 11, Nos. 5–6 (July–August 1990), p. 1415

9. See *Reconstructing Individualism: Autonomy, Individuality and the Self in Western Thought*, ed. by T. C. Heller, M. Sosna and D. Wellbery (Stanford, Calif.: Stanford University Press, 1986).

10. E. H. Erikson, *Childhood and Society* (New York, 1963); N. Sanford, *Self and Society* (New York, 1966); G. and R. Blank, "Toward a Psychoanalytic Developmental Psychology," in: *Journal of the American Psychoanalytic Association* (1972), pp. 668–710; Jane Loewinger, "The Meaning and Measurement of Ego Development," in: *American Psychologist*, 21 (1966), pp. 195–206.

11. F. R. Ankersmit, "Historiography and Postmodernism," in: *History and Theory*, Vol. 28, No. 2 (1989), pp. 137–53, here 144. Emmanuel Le Roy Ladurie's *Montaillou* seems to me a good illustration of postmodernist historiography. Would Fraser think that there are no differences that make a difference between the kind of approaches collected in the anthology *Becoming Visible. Women in European History*, ed. by R. Bridenthal, C. Koonz and S. Stuard (Boston: Houghton Mifflin, 1987) and the narrative of *Montaillou*?

12. See Joan Scott's review of *Heroes of their Own Lives. The Politics and History of Family Violence* by Linda Gordon; and Linda Gordon's review of Joan Scott's *Gender and the Politics of History*, in *Signs*, Vol. 15, No. 4 (Summer 1990), 848–60.

13. *Ibid.*, p. 849.

14. *Ibid.*, p. 850.

15. *Ibid.*, p. 851.

16. In her response to these objections, Nancy Fraser seems to imply that I am suggesting a forced choice, an either/or alternative among these paradigms; there is also the implication that I may be dismissing Joan Scott's tremendous contributions to feminist historiography and women's history. Absolutely not! I have learned a tremendous amount from the work of both scholars; only, I find myself in very serious disagreement with Joan Scott when she moves to a metatheoretical level and teases out an epistemology or social theory from her historiographic commitments. I think that in some of these considerations, Scott follows an honorable tradition of social scientists who, beginning with Max Weber, often practice one thing in their actual social research and say something different in their methodological reflections on this research.

17. Thomas McCarthy gives a very sensitive account of the development and transformations of Foucault's views of selfhood and agency in "The Critique of Impure Reason: Foucault and the Frankfurt School," in: *Ideals and Illusions. On Reconstruction and Deconstruction in Contemporary Critical Theory* (Cambridge, Mass.: MIT Press, 1991), pp. 67 ff.

18. The social-scientific deficits of Foucault's work—his inadequate conceptions of social action and social movements, his inability to explain social change except as the discontinuous displacement of one "power/knowledge" regime by another, and his thin concepts of self and identity-formation—are ultimately related. These problems have been at the center of the critical reception of Foucault's work in Germany in particular, whereas in the U.S Foucault has been read less as a social and cultural historian and social theorist, and more as a philosopher and literary critic. The result has been an uncritical reception of Foucault's explanatory framework. In her article "Foucault on Modern Power: Empirical Insights and Normative Confusions," first published in *Praxis International* (reproduced in *Unruly Practices* (Minneapolis: University of Minnesota Press, 1989), pp. 17–34), Nancy Fraser very early on drew attention to these difficulties in Foucault's work. An excellent analysis of Foucault's sociological assumptions, and particularly of his theory of modernity, can be found in Axel Honneth, *Kritik der Macht. Reflexionsstufen einer kritischen Gesellschaftstheorie* (Frankfurt: Suhrkamp, 1985), pp. 169–225, trans. by Kenneth Baynes, as *The Critique of Power. Reflective Stages in a Critical Social Theory* (Cambridge, Mass.: MIT Press, 1992)

19. Linda Gordon, "Response to Scott," p. 852.

20. This essay was first published in *Dissent* as "Sex-Discrimination Law and Equivalent Rights," [Summer 1991, pp. 400ff.] and included in the German original of our exchange with the title "Gender, *Geschlecht und gleichwertige Rechte.*" See Benhabib, Butler, Cornell and Fraser, *Der Streit um Differenz* (Frankfurt: Fischer, 1994), pp. 80–105. I have expanded my original remarks so as to take into account Cornell's new contribution to this volume, "What is Ethical Feminism?".

21. In "Democracy and Difference. The Metapolitics of Lyotard and Derrida" (*Journal of Political Philosophy*, vol. 2, No. 1 (1994), pp. 1–23) I have given a more detailed examination of some of Derrida's recent political writings.

22. See "Bowers v. Hardwick" (October 1985), *United States Reports,* vol. 478. Justice White writes: "The case does not require a judgment on whether laws against sodomy between consenting adults in general, or between homosexuals in particular, are wise or desirable . . . The issue presented is whether the Federal Constitution confers a fundamental right upon *homosexuals to engage in sodomy* and hence invalidates the laws of the many States that still make such conduct illegal and have done so for a very long time. . . . none of the rights announced in those cases [cases dealing with the privacy of the rights of marriage, procreation, etc. are meant—SB] bears any resemblance to the claimed constitutional right of homosexuals to engage in acts of sodomy that is asserted in this case." 478 U.S., pp. 190–191.

23. See Nancy Chodorow, *Feminism and Psychoanalytic Theory* (New Haven and London: Yale University Press, 1989), and in particular the chapters on "Gender, Relation and Difference in Psychoanalytic Perspective," "Feminism, Femininity and Freud," and Jessica Benjamin, *The Bonds of Love. Psychoanalysis, Feminism and the Problem of Domination,* (New York: Pantheon Books, 1988). The source of my continuing skepticism toward Lacanian psychoanalysis is the fact that Lacan does not analyze the woman as the subject of psycho-sexual development, but only addresses male fantasies about the woman, and probes the creation of the female for the purposes of the male imaginary. I am persuaded by the argument of feminist psychoanalytic theorists that male and female psychosexual developments are not symmetrical, and that gender asymmetries cannot simply be "worked into" the Lacanian framework from the outside as it were. It puzzles me why Cornell is so impervious to this issue in her continuing reliance upon the Lacanian framework. See Teresa Brennan, ed. *Between Feminism and Psychoanalysis* (New York: Routledge, 1989), and in particular pp. 8 ff. for

an exploration of some of these issues. See also Jane Flax's critique of Lacan in *Thinking Fragments*, pp. 100 ff.

24. See Drucilla Cornell, *Beyond Accommodation. Ethical Feminism, Deconstruction and the Law* (New York: Routledge, 1991); and *Philosophy of the Limit* (New York: Routledge, 1992).

25. I have dealt with the problem of value differentiation under conditions of modernity in *Critique, Norm and Utopia. A Study of the Foundations of Critical Theory* (New York: Columbia University Press, 1986), pp. 256 ff.

26. See Cornell's early article, "Feminism, Negativity, Inter-subjectivity," coauthored with Adam Thurschwell, in: *Feminism as Critique*, ed. by Benhabib and Cornell (Minnesota: Polity Press, 1897), pp. 143ff; and my *Critique, Norm and Utopia*, pp. 327ff.

27. See in particular my Introduction and pp. 148–178 in *Situating the Self. Gender, Community and Postmodernism in Contemporary Ethics* (Routledge, 1992).

28. See Seyla Benhabib, *Critique, Norm and Utopia. A Study of the Foundations of Critical Theory* (New York: Columbia University Press, 1986) and *Situating the Self. Gender, Community and Postmodernism* (London: Polity Press, 1992).

29. See Judith N. Shklar, *Legalism. An Essay on Law, Morals and Politics* (Cambridge, Mass.: Harvard University Press, 1964), p. 224.

30. See the series edited by S. N. Eisenstadt, *Patterns of Modernity*, volume 1, *The West* (New York: New York University Press, 1987).

6

For a Careful Reading

Judith Butler

March, 1994:

As a postscript to the essay written in September of 1990, I would like to respond to the criticisms articulated by both Seyla Benhabib and Nancy Fraser and offer some remarks in response to Drucilla Cornell's contributions to this volume. In some ways, the publication of these essays in 1995 seems already outdated. "Contingent Foundations" was a lecture I wrote in a polemical style and it is not one that I would write again today in the same way. At the time I understood myself to be embattled: what I understood to be an unreasoned and anxious response to the entry of poststructuralist discourse into feminist theory was, I thought, to be countered through a reasoned set of rejoinders to the complaint.

But what I have come to understand is that what I should have known all along, namely, that the pursuit of the reasonable is, as Nietzsche knew, the site and instrument of other kinds of investments, ones which are difficult, if not impossible, to uncover, much less to change. But because this thesis is not avowed, there is a deadlock that pervades this debate. This is, of course, a sad state of affairs. And, in the end, I find the work of this volume to be saddening. In a way, what structures this volume remains unspeakable within the very terms in which the volume proceeds. For the question of whether or not a position is right, coherent, or interesting is, in this case, less informative than why it is we come to occupy and defend the territory that we do, what it promises us, from what it promises to protect us. Unfortunately, this conversation is not one that takes place within the context of this volume.

In the place of a debate in which we might be open to a set of inquiries that call into question our most unreasoned attachments to the grounds or presuppositions of our way of thinking, we have more often engaged a kind of "position taking" in which one defends against the claims of the other and refuses to learn what is at stake in the making of the claim. And here I have been as culpable as the next. I found myself reading Paul Gilroy's *The Black Atlantic*[1] and taking note of the interesting use to which he puts Benhabib's defense of the narrative of modernity. Whereas he concedes that the narrative of modernity associated with European conceptions of emancipation have required and instituted slavery, and that the institution appears to undermine the claims made on behalf of an emancipatory trajec- tory for history, he also makes clear that struggle to overcome slav- ery makes important and vital use of that very emancipatory narrative. This strikes me as a position which, on the one hand, con- cedes the exclusionary force by which the "emancipatory" narrative of modernity proceeds, but, on the other hand, insists that that nar- rative is, as it were, open to a recontextualization and resignification that works to overcome that very exclusion. Significantly for me, this is a position which insists *both* on the exclusionary effects of the modernist narrative and the revisable and rearticulable status of that narrative as a cultural resource that has serviced a collective project of extending and enhancing human freedoms. Where Gilroy appears to depart from Benhabib is in treating the narrative of modernity as a cultural resource, a resignifiable tradition, one which has an histori- cal usefulness, but which is not grounded in a transcendental account of language or its implicit or ultimate set of aims. Perhaps one would call this a pragmatic appropriation of modernism, but it is, perhaps most importantly, one which affirms the political usefulness of the *de*-contextualization of such narratives, the condition of possibility for their *re*-contextualization: appropriation of a narrative for a po- litical purpose for which it was explicitly not devised. I would affirm the importance of such a (mis)appropriation in the context of con- temporary politics. And I would emphasize that the appropriation of a "foundation" affirms its postfoundational usefulness.

For what is at hand politically is a set of challenges that are histor- ically provisional, but are not for that reason any less necessary to engage. Indeed, I would suggest that a fundamental mistake is made when we think that we must sort out philosophically or epistemologically our "grounds" before we can take stock of the world politically or engage in its affairs actively with the aim of transformation. The claim that every political action has its theoretical presuppositions is not the same as the claim that such presuppositions must be sorted out prior to action. It may be that those presuppositions are articulated only in and through that action and become available only through a reflective posture made possible through that articulation in action. To set the "norms" of political life in advance is to prefigure the kinds of practices which will qualify as the political and it is to seek to negotiate politics outside of a history which is always to a certain extent opaque to us in the moment of action.

To set norms, to affirm aspirations, to articulate the possibilities of a more fully democratic and participatory political life is, nevertheless, a necessity. And I would claim the same for the contested status of "universality." In this sense, I am productively antagonized by the point offered by Helga Geyer-Ryan in her *Fables of Desire*[2] that "a virulent critique of covertly limited universality can only ever possess a rhetorical character" (181) and later, in terms which echo Gilroy's, "the partisan distortion and impoverishment of these concepts in the interests of patriarchal dominion should not be confused with the emancipatory power which these concepts articulated in the eighteenth century and which they continue to possess today." (191) Although I question the implicit equation of the rhetorical with the semantically empty, I would concede that "universality" ought to be subject to a radical misappropriation. The problem emerges, though, that what one means by "the universal" will vary, and the cultural articulation of that term in its various modalities will work against precisely the trans-cultural status of the claim. This is not to say that there ought to be no reference to the universal or that it has become, for us, an impossibility.[3] On the contrary. All this means is that there are cultural conditions for articulation which are not always the same, and that the term gains its meaning for us precisely through the decidedly less-than-universal cultural conditions of its articulation. This is a paradox that any injunction to adopt a universal attitude will encounter.

It may be that in one culture a set of rights are considered to be universally endowed, and that in another those very rights mark the limit to universalizability, i.e. "if we grant those people those rights we will be undercutting the foundations of the universal as we know it." This has become especially clear to me in the field of lesbian and gay human rights where "the universal" is a contested term, and where various cultures and various mainstream human rights groups voice doubt over whether lesbian and gay humans ought properly to be included in "the human" and whether their putative rights fit within the existing conventions governing the scope of rights considered universal.

Consider that to claim that there are existing conventions that govern the scope of rights considered to be universal is not the same as to claim that the scope of universal rights has been decided once and for all. In fact, it may be that the universal is only partially articulated, and that we do not yet know what form it will take. In this sense, the contingent and cultural character of the existing conventions governing the scope of universality does not deny the usefulness or importance of the term "universal." It simply means that the claim of universality has not yet received a full or final articulation and that it remains to be seen how and whether it will be articulated further. Indeed, it may well be politically important to claim that a given set of rights are universal even when existing conventions governing the scope of universality preclude precisely such a claim. Such a claim runs the good risk of provoking a radical rearticulation of universality itself. Whether the claim is preposterous, provocative, or efficacious depends on the collective strength with which it is asserted, the institutional conditions of its assertion and reception, and the unpredictable political forces at work. But the uncertainty of its success is not enough of a reason not to make the claim.

When competing claims to the universal are made, it seems imperative to understand that cultures do not exemplify a ready-made universal, but that the universal is always culturally articulated, and that the complex process of learning how to read that claim is not something any of us can do outside of the difficult process of cultural translation. This translation will not be an easy one where we reduce every cultural instance to a presupposed universality, nor will it be the enumeration of radical particularisms between which no communication is possible. The task that cultural difference sets for us is the articulation of universality through a difficult labor of translation, one in which the terms made to stand for one another are transformed in the process, and where the movement of that unanticipated transformation establishes the universal as that which is yet to be achieved and which, in order to resist domestication, may never be fully or finally achievable.

What any of those terms will mean, however, will not be determinable outside of the conflicts, institutional arrangements, and historical conditions in which they emerge. The lure of a transcendental guarantee, the promise of philosophy to "correct existence," in the sense that Nietzsche ironically imagined, is one which seduces us away from the lived difficulty of political life. This urge to have philosophy supply the vision that will redeem life, that will make life worth living, this urge is the very sign that the sphere of the political has *already* been abandoned. For that sphere will be the one in which those very theoretical constructions—those without which we imagine we cannot take a step—are in the very process of being lived as ungrounded, unmoored, in tatters, but also, as recontextualized, reworked, in translation, as the very resources from which a postfoundational politics is wrought. Indeed, it is their ungroundedness which is the condition of our contemporary agency, the very condition for the question: which way should we go?

It is that continuing need to literalize the ground, that sure anchor, that transcendental and, hence, fundamentally religious consolation, that keeps us from learning, from being able to hear, and to read how it is that we might now live politically *in medias res*. Indeed, it would be as much a mistake to elect "poststructuralism" as that sure ground as it would be to elect "quasi-transcendental pragmatics." And by living the political *in medias res*, I do not mean living the political as pure flux or as ceaseless change. That is, of course, as impossible as it is undesirable. Here is perhaps where Drucilla Cornell's emphasis on "transformation" is central: how is it that we become available to a transformation of who we are, a contestation which compels us to rethink ourselves, a reconfiguration of our "place" and our "ground," if we demand, in advance, to know that, as subjects, we are intact, uneroded, uncontested, presupposed, and necessary? Is such knowledge a political need, or is it the very stuff of political defensiveness, territorialism, the foreclosure of that future that constitutes the necessary opacity of what we are, and the guarantee of insuperable conflict as a way of life? What notion of "agency" will that be which always and already knows its transcendental ground, and speaks only and always from that ground? To be so grounded is nearly to be buried: it is to refuse alterity, to reject contestation, to decline that risk of self-transformation perpetually posed by democratic life: to give way to the very impulse of conservatism.

The bulk of what is written below as a "response" was completed in February, 1993. It seems to me that the disagreements which exist among us as thinkers are perhaps less salient than others which now hold sway in public intellectual life. I'm struck in many ways by what now appears to me to be the parochialism of these debates, for the four of us certainly are not representative of "feminism" or "feminist theory" as it is currently articulated. Missing from this volume is a sustained discussion of the place of racial difference in contemporary feminist debate; the ethical and political questions raised by reproductive rights and technologies; the ethical and political questions raised by the discourse of victimization which seems to prevail in U.S. public feminist debate and exemplified in the work of Catharine MacKinnon; the contemporary theoretical divergences between sexuality and gender studies initiated by lesbian and gay studies, the transnational problems of translating feminist political goals and their claim to "universality"; the remapping of power by feminist theory in ways that encompass shifting geopolitical terrains; the feminization and racialization of poverty both domestically and abroad.

Neither does this volume address the "theory wars," for, as a group, we toil in the domain of philosophy and its critique, and in that way dwell within a presupposed sense that theoretical reflection matters. As a result, though, the important questions raised concerning the rarefied status of theoretical language, the place of narrative in or as theory, the possibility of a theoretical activism, the tension between theory and empiricism, the question of whether poststructuralism is the only theory that counts as "theory," are not interrogated here.

None of the issues that are addressed here can be resolved by deciding for or against "the subject," for or against "modernity" or "progressive history," for or against "the transcendental norm." Those notions have entered into an historical crisis that no amount of reflection can reverse. It would, then, be a mistake to come away from this volume thinking that this constitutes a "debate" on the value or viability of any of those terms; the question here has much more to do with the question of whether any of those terms can serve as "grounds," or whether their continuing volatility is a sure sign that they have lost their ground, but retained their force with ambivalent consequences.

February, 1993:

What follows is a point by point rejoinder which I hope will further clarify what is at stake in the debate. This debate is *not* a debate between postmodernism and social criticism because there is no one who is claiming to "defend" postmodernism. I do not consider my work to be "postmodern," and indeed, I tried to explain in the essay some of the reasons why that term is not appropriate to what I propose. What is at stake in the first instance are certain presuppositions of *foundationalism*, whether they can be secured in advance and philosophically, and at what cost. In the second instance, what is of importance is recasting *agency within matrices of power*.

With respect to the question of foundations, I would maintain that they are (1) contingent and indispensable and (2) delimited and secured through certain exclusionary moves. In this sense, I am not an "anti-foundationalist." On the other hand, the effort to read past what I write in order to line me up with a caricature of the "postmodern" and the "anti-foundational" is, I think, interesting to read as a defensive intellectual posture. For there appears to be a resistance to reading, and to reading closely, in the effort to produce a monolith called "postmodernism" of which I then become a mere symptom. I hope that what follows will make it more difficult to impose that falsifying construction.

For Benhabib, on "Agency"

Benhabib writes that "Butler ... maintains ... we must bid farewell to the 'doer beyond the deed'" which is a literal misreading, for the text in my book and in Nietzsche's *Genealogy of Morals* reads, "the doer *behind* the deed" (my emphasis). She then proceeds to quote correctly, "there is no gender identity behind the expressions of gender; that identity is performatively constituted by the very 'expressions' that are said to be its results." (140)[4] Benhabib then goes on to attribute to me "a theory of the self" based on the above quotation, although the quotation itself only supports a limited version of my theory of *gender*. Indeed, if I were to offer a "theory of the self," which I do not, it would not be reducible to a theory of gender. And yet, Benhabib proceeds as if they were one: "Is there any possibility," she asks, "of changing those 'expressions' that constitute us?" In the course of *Gender Trouble*, I suggest that change and alteration is part of the very process of "performativity." Here Benhabib chooses not to consider what meaning of performativity is at work, and proceeds to reduce "performative constitution" to a behaviorist model in which the term "expressions" are said to construct or fashion a social self (Goffman appears to be the model for such a theory). The notion of performativity that I use, however, is one that runs directly counter to the one that Benhabib describes as "we are no more than the sum total of the gendered expressions we perform" (140).

The term "performativity" in my usage is taken from J. L. Austin's *How to Do Things with Words* and read through Derrida's "Signature, Event, Context" in *Limited, Inc.* as well as Paul de Man's notion of "metalepsis" articulated throughout his essays on Nietzsche in *Allegories of Reading*. A performative act is one which brings into being or enacts that which it names, and so marks the constitutive or productive power of discourse. To the extent that a performative appears to "express" a prior intention, a doer *behind* the deed, that prior agency is only legible *as the effect* of that utterance. For a performative to work, it must draw upon and recite a set of linguistic conventions which have traditionally worked to bind or engage certain kinds of effects. The force or effectivity of a performative will be derived from its capacity to draw on and reencode the historicity of those conventions in a present act. This power of recitation is not a function of an individual's *intention*, but is an effect of historically sedimented linguistic conventions. In "Signature, Event, Context," Derrida links the notion of performativity to *citation* and *repetition*: "could a performative utterance succeed if its formulation did not repeat a 'coded' or iterable utterance, or in other words, if the formula I pronounce in order to open a meeting, launch a ship or a marriage were not identifiable as *conforming* with an iterable model, if it were not then identifiable in some way as a 'citation'?" He writes further, "in such a typology, the category of intention will not disappear; it will have its place, but from that place it will no longer be able to govern the entire scene and system of utterance." (SEC, 18)

In other words, when words engage actions or constitute themselves a kind of action, they do this not because they reflect the power of an individual's will or intention, but because they draw upon and reengage conventions which have gained their power precisely through *a sedimented iterability*. The category of "intention," indeed, the notion of "the doer" will have its place, but this place will no longer be "behind" the deed as its enabling source. If the subject—a category within language and, hence, distinct from what Benhabib will call a "self"—is performatively constituted, then it follows that this will be a constitution *in time*, and that the "I" and the "we" will be neither fully determined by language nor radically free to instrumentalize language as an external medium.

To be constituted by language is to be produced within a given network of power/discourse which is open to resignification, redeployment, subversive citation from within, and interruption and inadvertent convergences with other such networks. "Agency" is to be found precisely at such junctures where discourse is renewed. That an "I" is founded through reciting the anonymous linguistic site of the "I" (Benveniste) implies that citation is not performed by a subject, but is rather the invocation by which a subject comes into linguistic being. That this is a repeated process, an iterable procedure, is *precisely* the condition of agency within discourse.[4] If a subject were constituted once and for all, there would be no possibility of a reiteration of those constituting conventions or norms. That the subject is that which must be constituted again and again implies that it is open to formations that are not fully constrained in advance. Hence, the insistence on finding agency *as* resignification in *Gender Trouble*: if the subject is a reworking of the very discursive processes by which it is worked, then "agency" is to be found in the possibilities of resignification opened up by discourse. In this sense, discourse is the horizon of agency, but also, performativity is to be rethought as resignification. There is no "bidding farewell" to the doer, but only to the *placement* of that doer "beyond" *or* "behind" the deed. For the deed will be itself and the legacy of conventions which it reengages, but also the future possibilities that it opens up; the "doer" will be the uncertain working of the discursive possibilities by which it itself is worked. This is doubtless related to Lacan's claim in *The Four Fundamental Concepts of Psychoanalysis* that every act is a repetition. In this sense, the "doer" will be produced as the effect of the "deed," but it will also constitute the dynamic hiatus by which further performative effects are achieved.

Benhabib misconstrues the theory of performativity I provide by grammatically reinstalling the subject "behind" the deed, and by reducing the above notion of performativity to theatrical performance: "If we are no more than the sum total of the gendered expressions we perform, is there ever any chance to stop the performance for a while, to pull the curtain down, and only let it rise if one can have a say in the production of the play itself?" I would argue that there is no possibility of standing *outside* of the discursive conventions by which "we" are constituted, but only the possibility of reworking the very conventions by which we are enabled. Gender performativity is not a question of instrumentally deploying a "masquerade," for such a construal of performativity presupposes an intentional subject *behind* the deed. On the contrary, gender performativity involves the difficult labor of deriving agency from the very power regimes which constitute us, and which we oppose. This is, oddly enough, *historical work*, reworking the historicity of the signifier, and no recourse to quasi-transcendental selfhood and inflated concepts of History will help us in this most concrete and paradoxical of struggles.

What does it mean to "situate" feminism at the same time that one makes fundamental to that feminism a de-situated transcendentalized self? Is this the solace that the philosopher needs in order to proceed, problematically imposed from the scene of philosophy onto the scene of politics? Is it right to suggest that any theory of agency must evacuate the situation of being discursively constituted and enabled in order to proceed?

Consider that according to one view of agency, a subject is endowed with a will, a freedom, an intentionality which is then subsequently "expressed" in language, in action, in the public domain. Here "freedom" and "the will" are treated as universal resources to which all humans *qua* humans have access. The self who is composed of such faculties or capacities is thus thwarted by relations of power which are considered external to the subject itself. And those who break through such external barriers of power are considered heroic or bearers of a universal capacity which has been subdued by oppressive circumstances. Whereas this emancipatory model of agency has surely been inspiring for many subordinated people, and for women in particular, it is crucial to consider the way in which this paradigm for thinking agency has come under question in recent years. Apart from the anthropological narrowness of the conception in which freedom or the will persist as universal invariants cross-culturally, there is no way to answer the question, "How does the construction of the subject as a bearer of emancipatory potential presuppose the very 'agency' that calls to be accounted for within complex interrelations of power, discourse, and practice?" In other words, what are the concrete conditions under which agency becomes possible, a very differ-

ent question than the metaphysical one, what is the sel
agency can be theoretically secured prior to any reference ι

What this means politically is that there is no opposition to pow
which is not itself part of the very workings of power, that agency is
implicated in what it opposes, that "emancipation" will never be the
transcendence of power as such.

Benhabib misconstrues the debate between historians Linda
Gordon and Joan W. Scott precisely on this point. Scott does not
argue that the women who seek recourse to the state to seek compensation for family violence lack agency; on the contrary, she asks what
it might mean to account for this agency that concrete relations of
discourse and power condition and limit the very possibility of making any such petition. As feminist theorists of the regulatory state
have made plain, the very bureaucracies through which women seek
compensation may also constitute the governmental means for re-
subordinating them. Hence, it is not a question of whether there is
evidence for agency in the materials that Gordon provides, but rather
how one accounts for the agency that exists. Is it to be inferred from
the structure of the self apart from its constitutive social and discursive relations, or will it be implicated from the start in the social and
discursive relations which both condition and limit the making of
any such claims? In the one view, agency is an attribute of persons,
presupposed as prior to power and language, inferred from the structure of the self; in the second, agency is the effect of discursive conditions which do not for that reason control its use; it is not a
transcendental category, but a contingent and fragile possibility
opened up in the midst of constituting relations. To claim that Scott
opposes agency is to refuse to read the challenge to theorize agency
that she provides. To claim that Scott understands women as only
erased is to miss the central point of her essay, namely, to ascertain
what constitutes agency within the very relations of power that constitute women as active beings. That the emotional stakes in this
reformulation are apparently so high is attested to by the fact that
Benhabib unaccountably fails to read the very passage from Scott
which she cites in her "Response" which makes Scott's position clear.

For Fraser, on "Critical Capacities"

Whereas Fraser appears to appreciate that there is a rethinking of
"agency" as resignification, she brings up two other questions. One

concerns the potential anti-humanism and esotericism of language I use such as, "power's own possibility of being reworked" and "signifying process." Such turns of phrase are remote from "everyday ways of talking and thinking," and so raise the question of whether such talk can have a political impact.

Here I would rejoin that it is probably not "esotericism" that is at issue for Fraser, whose own language is filled with Habermasian and Frankfurt School locutions which are equally remote from "everyday ways of talking and thinking." Indeed, if I understand the linguistic turn in Habermas, and Fraser's shared concern with asking after "warrants" and "validity," it relies on the premise that *ordinary language cannot provide ultimate grounds for adjudicating the validity of its own claims* (the implicit presuppositions of ordinary language need to be made explicit through a quasi-transcendental reflection which is decidedly unordinary). If I am right that that is precisely Fraser's point of view as well as the basis for her call for normative grounding, then she is plainly contradictory to use "ordinary language" as the ground from which she assesses the probable political impact of my prose.

Discourse is not merely spoken words, but a notion of signification which concerns not merely how it is that certain signifiers come to mean what they mean, but how certain discursive forms articulate objects and subjects in their intelligibility. In this sense, "discourse" is not used in the ordinary sense, but draws from the work of Foucault. Discourse does not merely represent or report on pregiven practices and relations, but it enters into their articulation and is, in that sense, productive.

In the course of formulating her second objection, Fraser claims that "'re-signification' carries . . . a positive charge" in my work, and asks why re-signification is good (172). In fact, my point is that re-signification is the domain in which a certain set of "agentic possibilities" can be discerned and derived, and that such a domain of possibility is *immanent* to power. My question is not whether certain kinds of significations are good or bad, warranted or unwarranted, but, rather: what constitutes the domain of discursive possibility within which and about which such questions can be posed? My argument is that "critique," to use Fraser's terms, always takes place *immanent* to the regime of discourse/power whose claims it seek to adjudicate, which is to say that the practice of "critique" is implicated in the very power-relations its seeks to adjudicate. There is no pure place outside of power by which the question of validity might be raised, and where validity is raised, it is also always an activity of power.

In what appears to be a separate objection, Fraser writes, "Like [Foucault], she insists that subjects are constituted through exclusion," and then she offers directly thereafter a phrase which is intended, it appears, as a paraphrase: "some people are authorized to speak authoritatively while others are silenced." (173) The paraphrase rests on a misreading of the above, for at stake for me is not who is authorized to speak, and who is de-authorized into silence. That formulation suggests that there are already subjects who are formed, some of whom are speaking, some of whom are silent and silenced. My question is how it is that a "subject" becomes formed at all, and here I would suggest that no "subject" comes into existence as a speaking being except through the repression of certain possibilities of speech (this is the significance of psychosis as unspeakable speech); moreover, subjects are formed through relations of *differentiation* (a position which I take from psychoanalysis and the relation between kinship, psychic formation, and language). The subject who emerges as a speaking being is able to cite itself as an "I," and provisionally to establish through exclusion the linguistic contours of its own "I-ness." The exclusionary formation of the "subject" is neither good nor bad, but rather, a psychoanalytic premise which one might usefully employ in the service of a political critique. For certain versions of the subject, understood as figures of mastery and instrumental will, have conventionally been marked as masculine and have required the de-subjectivation of the feminine. This is one politically consequential permutation of the exclusionary formation of the subject, but it is not the only one. And the questions that Fraser asks about that formation are, in fact, ones which I would happily adopt as my own: "Can we overcome or at least ameliorate the asymmetries in current practices of subjectivation? Can we construct practices, institutions, and forms of life in which the empowerment of some does not entail the disempowerment of others? If not, what is the point of feminist struggle?" (173)

Nicholson raises this question in her introduction, asking how it is that I can, on feminist grounds, object to the exclusionary formation of the subject and then claim that the exclusionary formation of the subject is neither good nor bad. It might be clarifying, then, to consider that whereas every subject is formed through a process of differentiation, and that the process of becoming differentiated is a necessary condition of the formation of the "I" as a bounded and distinct kind of being, that there are better and worse forms of differentiation, and that the worse kinds tend to abject and degrade those from whom the "I" is distinguished. I tried to consider this problem of abjection in *Bodies That Matter* and have tried as well to explore the melancholic consequences for ego-formation of a differentiation that takes the form of disavowal.[5] If the "I" that I am requires the abjection of others, then this "I" is fundamentally dependent on that abjection; indeed, that abjection is installed as the condition of this "I" and constitutes that posture of autonomy as internally weakened by its own founding disavowals. My objection to this form of disavowal is that it weakens the sense of self, establishes its ostensible autonomy on fragile grounds, and requires a repeated and systematic repudiation of others in order to acquire and maintain the appearance of autonomy. This means, of course, that I oppose repudiation and abjection as the means by which an ostensible "autonomy" is produced, and I have tried in the above-mentioned text to trace some of the more lamentable consequences of that process in the occasionally rancorous articulation of identity politics. My call, then, is for the development of forms of differentiation which lead to fundamentally more capacious, generous, and "unthreatened" bearings of the self in the midst of community. That an "I" is differentiated from another does not mean that the other becomes unthinkable in its difference, nor that the other must become stucturally homologous to the "I" in order to enter into community with that "I." At the level of political community, what is called for is the difficult work of cultural translation in which difference is honored without (a) assimilating difference to identity or (b) making difference an unthinkable fetish of alterity.

And if one then wants to know, but how would I *ground* the claim that such a community is better than one based on repudiation and abjection, it seems important to remember that whatever ground one might offer would have to be communicated and, hence, become subject to the same labor of cultural translation that it is being asked to ground.

Finally, then, Fraser asks whether certain kinds of foundationalism have not had emancipatory effects, and if they have, does not that constitute a good political reason to retain foundationalism. She gives as her example "the French Revolution and the appropriation of its foundationalist view of subjectivity by the Haitian 'Black Jacobin,' Toussaint de l'Ouverture." (173) But here Fraser's example makes my point, for if Toussaint de l'Ouverture "appropriates" a foundationalist view of subjectivity from the French Revolution, then that "view" is taken and redeployed, "re-signified" in Haitian terms; taken from elsewhere, deployed strategically, that view of subjectivity is precisely *not* a foundation, not there from the start, not presupposed, but instituted through a subversive citation and redeployment. This is then a "foundation" that moves, and which changes in the course of that movement, and I am in favor of that precisely because I see possibility therein.

It is clear that in order to set political goals, it is necessary to assert normative judgements. In a sense, my own work has been concerned to expose and ameliorate those cruelties by which subjects are produced and differentiated. I concede that this is not the only goal, and that there are questions of social and economic justice which are not primarily concerned with questions of subject-formation. To this end it is crucial to rethink the domain of power-relations, and to develop a way of adjudicating political norms without forgetting that such an adjudication will also always be a struggle of power.

March, 1994:
For Cornell, on the Other

Cornell has reread Lacan in an Irigarayan vein, claiming that the "feminine" within the masculine symbolic is incommensurable with the "feminine" as it exists outside and beyond those symbolic parameters.[6] The dialectic of recognition that we might expect from two symetrically positioned subjects is, thus, not a possibility between "the masculine" and the "feminine," for the "feminine" will always be erased by the symbolic position of lack into which it is placed. Thus, in a move which appears at first to be in tension with received notions of equality, Cornell will argue that ethical recognition will always consist in a failure to comprehend the other. The limit of recognition in the sense of comprehension is, paradoxically, the advent of ethical recognition, understood as the recognition of the limits of comprehensibility.

Thus, Cornell repositions both the "masculine" and the "feminine" as symbolic positions, ones which acquire their significance for us within the terms of a systematic asymmetry. On the one hand, I agree with Cornell that both the "masculine" and the "feminine," strictly speaking, do not exist: they do not belong to the realm of reality. It is in this sense that Cornell will argue that the feminine is an "impossibility," but one which continues to exert its force and meaning in the domain of reality. I agree with her to the extent that I understand femininity to be an impossible ideal, on which compels a daily mime that can, by definition, never succeed in its effort to approximate that ideal. I would, on the other hand, underscore that these governing "impossibilities" are socially produced in complex ways, and would question whether the Lacanian scheme of symbolic and imaginary can account for the complex and divergent ways in which these impossible ideals are manufactured and sustained.

In my view, these idealizations are underwritten by figures of abjection which do not make an appearance within the array of symbolic positions articulated by Lacan. How is that symbolic circumscribed, and through what exclusions? What counts as an "intelligible" identity, and is it only "the feminine" that operates within the symbolic domain as the sign of its limit and impossibility? To the extent that the symbolic encodes a set of idealizations, it is constituted by the imaginary that it claims to govern. In this sense, the symbolic is nothing other than the reification of a given imaginary, and, in the case of Lacan, that is the heterosexual imaginary. Neither the "masculine" nor "the feminine" in his sense can be sustained without the presupposition of the structural asymmetry of heterosexuality. What does it mean to be "outside" or "beyond" both the "masculine" and the "feminine" in this sense? That region is yet to be mapped, but its mapping will demand a rethinking of the governing power of the symbolic as the heterosexualizing prerequisite by which the viability of the subject, masculine or feminine, is linguistically instituted.

My sense is that we must begin to think the convergence and reciprocal formation of various imaginaries, and that sexual difference is neither more primary than other forms of social difference, nor is its formation understandable outside of a complex mapping of social power.

Like Cornell, I understand the deconstructive notion of "the constitutive outside" to be central to a critical understanding of how the subject is formed, how the symbolic as limiting horizon is established, and how politics is thus obliged to move beyond an analysis of what is already given. What is "outside" is not simply the Other—

the "not me"—but a notion of futurity—the "not yet"—and these constitute the defining limit of the subject itself. But this notion of the "constitutive outside" has another valence as well: the unspeakable, the unrepresentable, the socially unintelligible. Is this "outside" what *cannot* or *ought not* to be represented or comprehended? The feminine, the sublime, or (and?) that which is too degraded and unthinkable to admit into the domain of representation: the abjected as such? It may be that this is the very question posed by the defining alterity, the question which establishes this limit as an ethical challenge: Will what appears as radically Other, as pure exteriority, be that which we refuse and abject as that which is unspeakably "Other," or will it constitute that limit that actively contests what we already comprehend and already are? This latter is the limit as the condition for our movement toward alterity, our potential transformation by virtue of that [and this] self-limiting encounter.

Notes

1. Cambridge, Mass.: Harvard University Press, 1993, pp. 1–41.

2. Cambridge, England and Cambridge, Mass.: Polity Press, 1994. See Chapter 11, "Enlightenment, Sexual Difference, and the Autonomy of Art".

3. See chapters 1, 3, and 7 in *Bodies That Matter: On the Discursive Limits of "Sex"* (New York: Routledge, 1993); see also "Melancholy Gender/Refused Identifications" in *Psychoanalytic Dialogues*, with reply by Adam Phillips, and response to reply, forthcoming, April 1995.

4. All pagination is from this volume.

5. I use discourse here in a Foucauldian vein, to be differentiated from "language" spoken or written, and from forms of representation and/or meaning-constitution. The discourse on subjects (whether it be a discourse of mental health, legal rights, criminality, sexuality) is constitutive of the *lived* and *actual* experience of such subjects, for it does not merely report on subjects, but comes to articulate the possibilities in which subjects achieve intelligibility, that is, in which subjects appear at all.

6. For a longer discussion of Drucilla Cornell's work, see my "Poststructuralism and Postmarxism," in *Diacritics* 23.4:3–11, Winter,

7

Rethinking the Time of Feminism

Drucilla Cornell

Judith Butler and I share a dream—a dream that clichés strung together, purportedly to give meaning to "something" called "postmodernism," will be disassociated from the diverse thinkers who have been branded as "postmodernists." I have argued that "postmodernism" is a term best saved to describe specific breaks with the high modernism of the avant-garde, and that these breaks must be carefully defined within the particular sphere of artistic endeavor under consideration. The term "postmodernism" should be separated from "postmodernity," when "postmodernity" is understood as an identifiable historical period with a "positive" set of characteristics that distinguish it from modernity. I even question "postmodernity's" adequacy as a description of either a set of hypotheses that can be associated with a specific group of thinkers or with a series of normative and political rejections that could successfully indicate a unique historical period.[1] I have also argued that thinkers who are frequently identified as postmodernists, such as Jacques Derrida and Emmanuel Lévinas, explicitly reject a concept of history which would accept this kind of rigid periodization.[2] But the basis for my concern is not simply the respect for textual fidelity that is an ethical concern remaining at the very heart of deconstruction, even when understood as a practice of reading.[3] The focus of my concern is that the very articulation of what "postmodernism" purportedly "is" obscures crucial issues in feminist theory. This articulation mistakenly identifies what is at stake in the debate among feminists who are aligned with postmodern thinkers, such as Butler and myself, and those like Seyla Benhabib, who remain tied to a particular interpretation of German Critical Theory. I agree completely with Nancy Fraser that no simple antithesis can or should be drawn between Critical Theory and so-called "postmodernism."

There is a fundamental alliance between my understanding of ethical feminism and a program of critical social investigation advocated in the earlier years of the Frankfurt School. Like Theodor Adorno and Max Horkheimer, I would insist that such a program of critical and social research integrate psychoanalysis. My recrafting is that within the context of feminism it must include an account of the dearth of symbolizations for the feminine within sexual difference, and why that dearth of symbolization must itself be explored as a crucial aspect of social research. In her characterization of my position as based on the use of psychoanalysis as foundational, Fraser misunderstands the "critical" role I attribute to my own appropriation of Lacan. Fraser fails to understand how unconscious motivation and the construction of social fantasy must be the basis of any critical social research program, one that would, of course, need to include historical investigation into the meaning of woman and women and how women have struggled to change their lot. Even the most technical tools of investigation of social reality, such as regression analysis, demand a careful account of how the variables at stake have been evaluated. This evaluation demands that we fully come to terms with unconscious motivation and social fantasy diverged by cultural contexts. Furthermore, there is nothing foundationalist or universalistic about this program of critical social research, particularly in my insistence that gender is best understood as an encoded system of stratified differentiation, incompatible with the historical shift in modernity to functional differentiation; that is, a historical analysis. In fact, my own understanding of critical social research is in deep sympathy with the ethical demand for sensitivity to cultural difference and historical diversity. Ironically, the lack of emphasis on unconscious motivation and social fantasy in empirical research can itself be analyzed as an aspect of a questionable Eurocentric assumption about the "nature" of social reality.[4] But in spite of my insistence on the centrality of a program of critical social research, the political and ethical aspirations of feminism cannot be reduced to such a program.

This leads me to another aspect of my disagreement with Fraser's interpretation of my critical appropriation of Lacan. Fraser argues that my purportedly "foundationalist," and thus ahistorical, account limits the possibilities of historical struggle. The opposite is the case: I turn Lacan's conclusions about the impossibility of feminism on their head and ethically reinterpret the possibility inherent in Lacan's assertion that there is no ground for Woman in the masculine symbolic. I believe that the feminine within sexual difference cannot be reduced to or philosophically limited by any of its current designations. Feminism demands nothing less than the unleashing of the feminine imaginary—an imaginary made possible, paradoxically, by the lack of grounding of the feminine in any of the identifications we know and imagine as Woman. My reinterpretation of the impossibility of Woman does not bind us to the logic of phallogocentrism, as Fraser suggests. Instead, it opens up endless possibilities for the reelaboration of sexual difference. Fraser also misunderstands my "conception" of language. My argument following Wittgenstein is that a linguistic field cannot be totalizing. I use my critical appropriation of Lacan to make the additional point that this failure of "totalization" can help us understand the unconcious without rooting it in the repressed drives. But does my insistence on the importance of psychoanalysis mean that I deny the significance of history?

Does it mean that I argue that there is no historical difference between societies in the possibilities for feminist political struggle? Of course not. We inevitably negotiate and indeed discover the possibilities of change through confronting the limits imposed upon us by our time. The word "feminist" is itself intimately related to the democratic revolutions in the West. But it is precisely the "westernization" of the term that has made some women of color suspicious that it cannot be separated from its Western roots, and more specifically from the imperialist imaginary. Thus, we are ethically called to investigate the historical meaning given to the category "feminism."

The claim that I ignore history misunderstands what I mean by the philosophy of the limit and its relevance to feminism. My philosophical point is only that any social, symbolic system does not and cannot foreclose altogether the possibility of women's resistance. This insight I have then applied to my analepsis of gender as a stratified system of gender differentiation that operates in cultures in which patriarchal lineage reinforces and expresses the Oedipal triangle.

Niklas Luhmann's system theory upon which I rely is neither totalizing, nor metaphysical.[5] Without philosophical reflection on how history is shaped by the categories in which it is invested we risk seeing resistance only in our own terms. As a result, we can fail to adequately assess or even *see* the struggles of women from different cultures and classes as struggles that "count" from a feminist perspective. Simply put, history is not just there; it is there as it is known. Philosophy helps us to reflect on how history comes to be known in part through the discounting of what is unworthy of study. Critical investigation into historical categories and the normative presuppositions smuggled into these categories mitigates against our blindness by demanding that we philosophically investigate the meaning of what we call history. Thus, I disagree with Fraser that we can neatly separate history from philosophy. Indeed, assessments of the possibility of resistance, and what counts as resistance, turn on normative presuppositions which should not be presumed, but must be justified. My argument is that we need philosophy for this justification and indeed for the argument that justification is necessary. I disagree with Fraser's argument that history is not a philosophical category and thus with her conclusion that feminism does not need philosophy. But what kind of philosophy, and what role should philosophy play in feminism?

Like Benhabib, I believe that feminism demands the thinking of the "wholly Other" and thus must retain, and proceed through, an unerasable moment of utopianism. On the other hand, I disagree with Benhabib that we can philosophically justify a description of a normative rational sphere upon which a theoretical reflection of morality can be based. Benhabib ultimately refuses the utopianism of the early Frankfurt School which turns on a similar distinction I have made between the ethical and moral. Benhabib's philosophical attempt to describe a normative rational sphere is inherently conservative within the context of feminism because feminism demands of us a constant challenge to the traditional philosophical delimitation of spheres upon which such theoretical reflections of morality have rested. Feminism demands nothing less than the creation of a feminine symbolic which feeds off the feminine imaginary and challenges the constraints of established discourse.

Feminism also should not establish itself on the basis of the foreclosure of the specificity of the feminine within sexual difference by reducing "it" to a "lack," to be filled by masculine fantasies. Rather, the feminine symbolic awaits us in the future, and will always remain in the future, because there can never be an end to its creation and recreation. The feminine within sexual difference can always be written precisely because the "being" of this difference is in its writing, its re-narrativization, and is never simply "there" in reality or as "it" has been represented by a masculine symbolic.[6] I take issue with Benhabib because she is not a utopian, in the specific sense that she thinks that feminism can operate within the philosophical tools provided by Habermas's attempt to theorize the legitimacy of a normative rational sphere of nature. Unlike the earlier thinkers of the Frankfurt School, such as Adorno and Walter Benjamin, Benhabib downplays the ethical and political significance of art, and more specifically, in the realm of social theory she ignores the importance of experimental writing styles which expose the operations of the masculine symbolic. No one emphasized the limit of traditional philosophical discourse in the expression of political critique more militantly than Theodor Adorno. Feminism is radical because it demands that we re-think the "origins" and the "limit" of philosophical discourse, even as we are challenged to do so philosophically, which is why feminism finds itself in alliance with thinkers such as Jacques Derrida and Emmanuel Lévinas, as well as with Adorno and Benjamin. But to see why there is the basis for such an alliance, we must re-articulate the philosophical positions that Benhabib, following Jane Flax, associates with "postmodernism."[7]

I replace Flax's categorizations with my own: First, The Significance of the Exposure of the Limit of Phallogocentrism. Second, The Significance of the Future Anterior and of Recollective Imagination[8] in the Comprehension of History. And last, The Significance of the Critique of the Era of the Ego. What I can provide in the short space allotted to me is only a stark sketch, but even so, I hope that this redefinition of the positions associated with so-called "postmodernism" will add new dimensions to the debate. In each case I will focus on the significance of my redefinition of the positions associated with "postmodernism" and the creation of a feminine symbolic.

I. The Significance of the Exposure of the Limit of Phallogocentrism

The "tall tale," which is how Benhabib describes Derrida's account of Western philosophy, involves an account of how philosophy "hardens" itself to its Other, and more specifically to the feminine

Other. As I argued in the essay included in this volume, the importance of Jacques Lacan's psychoanalytic theory for Derrida is that it provides the most compelling account of how the structures of conscious language are inherently, through a unconscious erasure of the feminine from the symbolic order, inseparable from the erasure of the significance of the Mother. This erasure takes place through the erection of the phallus as the transcendental signifier, which cements meaning through the privileging of the masculine. The erection of the phallus as the transcendental signifier gives operational cultural force to the fantasy that to have a penis is to have the phallus, with all its supposed magical qualities of creation and potency. The fantasy that the phallus is the only symbol of re-generation lies at the basis of patrilineal lineage and of patriarchy.

Lacan's symbolic re-interpretation of the Oedipal complex demonstrates the unconscious significance of the Name of the Father at the level of cultural work, including the work of philosophy. The feminist significance of fighting patrilineal lineage on behalf of the realization of a democracy not based on the system of stratified differentiation inherent in patriarchy has been brought to the center stage by "third"-world women. An example is the politicization of the role of the Queen Mothers in Ghana, who have publicized the relationship between the challenge to patrilineal lineage and the possibility of a true participatory democracy. A crucial aspect of this struggle against the unconscious identification of the phallus with reproductive power demands the re-symbolization and re-evaluation of the feminine "sex." In her extraordinary novel, *Possessing The Secret of Joy,*[9] Alice Walker retells the story of how the feminine "sex" comes to be symbolized as dolls, in order to allegorize the horrifying process by which patriarchal culture tames what it most fears—a fully grown woman whose "sex" is celebrated rather than mutilated. The secret of joy, resistance, is inseparable from this symbolic battle against the unconscious significance given to the phallus as reproductive power. The erasure of the feminine "sex" is enacted in the ritual which makes the "lack" of woman a horrifying reality.

> We are not supposed to have vaginas under this scheme, says Olivia, with a smartness of speech that sometimes characterizes her, because it is through that portal that man confronted the greatest undeserved mystery known to him. Himself reproduced.[10]

The great fantasy of the phallus is that it does not need its Other, which is why there remains a profound connection—a connection of which Butler reminds us—between certain philosophical depictions of the ideal of autonomy and the myth of autogenesis in which Man produces himself rather than is reproduced. When Derrida entitled one of his texts *Dissemination*,[11] he was providing us with an important reminder of how productive the penis is when there is no Other to receive it.

Derrida, of course, does not engage in the process of the resymbolization of the feminine with sexual difference in the same way that a novelist like Alice Walker does. But his exposure of the limit of phallogocentrism—the way in which central philosophical concepts are profoundly tied in with the unconscious significance given to the phallus—is an important intervention for making that process of resymbolization possible. The story of how the phallus comes to be read as the transcendental signifier, and how it stands in for the power of reproduction, is a tall tale indeed. Derrida believes that the phallus is erected only as the transcendental signifier through a reading of what the mother desires, and that her desire is read within a pre-given script that translates desire through the grid of the already established symbolic. But what is read can always be reread. On the level of philosophical conceptualization, this re-reading demands that we resymbolize our most basic concepts such as autonomy. As Walker's novel reminds us, there can be no "autonomy" for women without the re-evaluation of our "sex" and with this re-revaluation the redefinition of the ideal of autonomy.

II. The Significance of the Future Anterior and of Recollective Imagination in History

This leads me to my second re-articulation of the positions associated with "postmodernism." Benhabib argues that even if we forsake metanarratives of the "history of man," we will still need accounts of how and why women have been oppressed. Yet she rejects the use of psychoanalysis in Joan Scott's path-breaking work which demonstrates the way in which what counts in "women's history," and indeed who counts as a "woman" in such a narrative demands a "deep" analysis of the social symbolic order in which the readings of Woman are made available.[12] Scott does not deny the reality of history or the suffering of women. She is demanding only that we heed the way in which the symbolic plays itself out in the stories of women's history that are given credibility as "true." Her studies demand that we look at the way Woman is constituted by the historians themselves as a meaningful and/or insignificant category.

Far from denying the politics of history and of the task of the historian, Scott brings politics to the fore with an implicit Lacanian understanding of the process of constitution of the *always already having been* through the future anterior. Scott understands that there is an inconclusive futurity of what will *always already have been*: a "time" which can never be entirely remembered, because even if read as *already constituted*, the past is being constituted even as it is read. The "interest in emancipation" in Scott's work is in making this "futurity" appear so as to make fluid the sedimentation of readings that give us a "past" that is purportedly just "there" as the *always already having been*.[13] This futurity, or the futural "past," is not easily defined as an interest in emancipation if the idea of emancipation cannot be given stable content. Instead, the most basic concepts of politics, such as emancipation, are themselves opened up at the same time that the category Woman is examined in the specificity of its variegated social-symbolic webs, including those inevitably imposed by the network of entangled meanings of "sex" that the historian brings to her own reading. Scott's work, with its Lacanian as well as its Derridean influences, exemplifies the recollective imagination in which what is remembered is envisioned differently as it is recollected in the reading of the historian. Scott's historical work is in this sense an important contribution to the creation of a feminine symbolic as it constantly challenges the definitions of Woman that have come to establish female identity, and which thus limit the reimagining of the feminine within sexual difference.

Lacan's understanding of the future anterior is a challenge to Hegel, who gives us the most powerful articulation of the subject of metaphysics in which the subject attains the self-contained form of presence—that of the present made perfect. I stress the political significance of Scott's historical studies to emphasize the way in which the understanding of temporality of the subject of history—and as we will see in a moment, of the individual subject that challenges the philosophy of presence—can help us re-articulate sexual difference beyond accommodation to the limits of the masculine symbolic.

III. The Significance of the Critique of the Era of the Ego

Lacan's concept of the future anterior means that the living present of the subject can reside only in an anticipated belatedness. Used modally, the future anterior designates a surmised conditional predication, and hence, a proposition bearing upon an uncertain state of affairs. This uncertainty, which cannot be identified simply with a future or a past, typifies the language of a subject whose self-consciousness is structured in terms of anticipated belatedness. In accordance with the split temporality of the future anterior, language will have been subject to, and become part of, the unconscious. The unconscious, must be understood not as an object of perception or intuition, and not as a clinical object, but as a theatrical scene that is in turn inscribed in an ongoing, if other scenario. The future anterior announces the disjunctive immediacy of this other scenario. If there is such a phenomenon as "postmodern" drama, it involves precisely this dramatization of the disjunctive immediacy of this other scenario, in which the very idea of characters in a shared present is challenged.

This understanding of temporality underlies Lacan's critique of ego psychology because Lacan chooses a synchronic perspective rather than the diachronic developmental point of view that has dominated orthodox psychoanalysis since Freud. Emphasisizing how the unconscious is generated, not only by the split temporality of the subject in time, but also by the displacement of meaning inherent in Saussure's understanding of how signs come to signify, differentiates Scott's approach to history from Fraser's positivism and exemplifies what I mean by a critical, historical social-research program.

There are two specific aspects of Lacan's critique of ego psychology that are crucial to feminism. Lacan's account of the ego is that the ego, and more specifically the bodily ego, is constituted by an Other who mirrors the infant as "whole," prior to her being able to achieve anything like bodily unity. This infant is dependent upon being mirrored and thus continuously reproduced through the eyes of the Other. A self understood as a self-constituting ego is based on a profound form of mis-recognition in which the ego comes "to be" by unconsciously taking up the place of the imaginary Other and then "forgets" the process of identification and interiorization of the Other which establishes the ego.

We can now understand from a different standpoint the significance of the subject being caught up in the future anterior—the subject will have been the image of the Other whose place it takes. But
in order to take the place of the imaginary Other, it must also repu-
diate the alterity of the futural past, and more specifically, as Walker
reminds us, the past of its *reproduction*. This is also Butler's point
when she emphasizes how the myth of autogenesis turns on the erasure of the Mother. There also is another aspect of the repudiation of
the alterity of the futural past which is important to feminism. For
Lacan, the denial of the irreducible alterity upon which the ego
depends takes place through the interiorization of the relationship of
the Other who mirrors the self. It is this interiorization which wipes
out the futural past that allows for the fantasy that the ego is self-
constituting in the present. The interiorization of the Other takes the
form of the psychical fantasy of Woman in which the otherness and
exteriority of actual women is denied. Thus, although Lacan is close
to Adorno in endlessly reminding us of the violence and aggression
inherent in the myth of autogenesis, he explicitly connects the interiorization of the Mother/Other to the reduction of Woman to fantasy
structures of the masculine psyche, in which the actual individuation
of women is denied and replaced with an unconscious fantasy object
with only two sides: good mother, evil whore.

The beginning of the other subject demands the recognition that
Woman is Other to the fantasy structures of the masculine psyche.
Thus, there is an ethical and political significance for feminism in the
recognition of the exteriority of the Other, including the exteriority
of the time frame of the futural past. The insistence of the ethical
recognition of the irreducible exteriority of the Other is, of course, at
the heart of Lévinas' concept of the subject who is always a subject
for the Other. In Derrida's *Glas*,[14] this recognition of the exteriority
of the Other takes place through the explicit recognition of the
futural past of the reproduction of the subject. The masculine subject
in *Glas* does not say "I am," but rather, "I follow, Her". This recognition of the futural past of the reproduction of the subject is not the
death of the subject, but the "birth" of a subject other to the ego.

I want to conclude with one more aspect of the political importance for feminism of the recognition of the subject in time. The
recognition of the time of the subject means that there is no self-identical subject—including the self-identical subject of feminism. But
this understanding of the subject does not mean that we have to

choose between the politics of identity or the politics of difference. This other subject returns us, instead, to the theatricality of the enactment of a mimetic identification as the basis for feminist politics, an enactment which is always toward the future, because it enacts as constituted what has yet to be. It is no coincidence that it is in the voices of African American slave women in Toni Morrison's *Beloved* who are utterly denied the subject position that we find the Other subject beautifully evoked in and through the very impossibility of achieving a self-constituted identity. This other subject is created as she is prayed for and mourned:

> Beloved
> You are my sister
> You are my daughter
> You are my face; you are me
> I have found you again; you have come back to me
> You are my Beloved
> You are mine
> you are mine
> you are mine.[15]

The time of feminism is the time of the future anterior of the Other, Beloved.

> You rememory me?
> Yes. I remember you
> You never forgot me?
> Your face is mine.[16]

Notes

1. See Drucilla Cornell, *The Philosophy of the Limit*, "What is Post-Modernity, Anyway?" (New York: Routledge, Chapman and Hall, 1992), pp. 1–12.

2. See Cornell, *The Philosophy of the Limit*, pp. 10–12.

3. See Cornell, *The Philosophy of The Limit*, pp. 81–83.

4. See Gananath Obeyesekere, *The Work of Culture: Symbolic Transformation in Psychoanalysis and Anthropology*, (Chicago: University of Chicago Press, 1990).

5. See Drucilla Cornell, "Enabling Paradoxes," unpublished manuscript on file with the author.

6. For my own attempt to re-define the political significance of feminine writing, see Drucilla Cornell, *Beyond Accommodation: Ethical Feminism, Deconstruction and the Law*, "Feminine Writing, Metaphor, and Myth", (New York: Routledge, Chapman and Hall, 1991), pp. 165–196.

7. See Seyla Benhabib, "Feminism and Post-Modernism: An Uneasy Alliance," (this volume). Teresa Brennan coined this phrase. I borrow it from her. See Teresa Brennan, *History after Lacan* (New York: Routledge, 1993). Brennan brilliantly argues that ego's era is itself historically circumscribed and specific. Thus, Brennan's answer to Fraser is that Lacan, or at least the crucial Lacanian critique of ego psychology, should be read as a historical thinker.

8. "Recollective imagination" is a phrase I have used for how the "past" operates in both our individual and collective histories. For a more detailed explanation of what I mean by recollective imagination, see Drucilla Cornell, *Transformations: Sexual Difference and Recollective Imagination*, (New York: Routledge, Chapman and Hall, forthcoming 1993).

9. Alice Walker, *Possessing The Secret of Joy*, (Florida: Harcourt Brace Jovanovich, 1992).

10. Walker, *Possessing The Secret of Joy*, p. 198.

11. Jacques Derrida, *Dissemination*, trans. Barbara Johnson (Chicago: University of Chicago Press, 1981). Originally published as *La Dissémination* (Paris: Editions du Seuil, 1972).

12. See generally Joan Wallach Scott, *Gender and The Politics of History* (New York: Columbia University Press, 1988). For Benhabib's critique of Scott, see *The Situated Self* (New York: Routledge, Chapman and Hall, 1992) pp. 221–222.

13. See Martin Heidegger, *On Time and Being*, trans. Joan Stambaugh (New York: Harper & Row, 1972), pp. 8–24.

14. Jacques Derrida, *Glas*, trans. John P. Leavey, Jr. and Richard Rand (Lincoln: University of Nebraska Press, 1986). Originally published as *Glas* (Paris: Editions Galilée, 1974).

15. Toni Morrison, *Beloved* (New York: Penguin Books, 1987), p. 216.

16. Morrison, *Beloved*, p. 215.

8

Pragmatism, Feminism, and the Linguistic Turn

Nancy Fraser

It is striking how many of the issues debated here concern signification and discourse. What began as an exchange about feminism and postmodernism has turned largely into a dispute about how best to interpret the linguistic turn. This development is not surprising. Feminists, like other theorists, work today in a context marked by the problematization of language. This, to my mind, is the most fruitful way of understanding postmodernism: an epochal shift in philosophy and social theory from an epistemological problematic, in which mind is conceived as reflecting or mirroring reality, to a discursive problematic, in which culturally constructed social meanings are accorded density and weight. Such a shift carries with it the condition diagnosed by Jean-François Lyotard. Belief in philosophical metanarratives tends to decline with the linguistic turn, since to accord density and weight to signifying processes is also to cast doubt on the possibility of a permanent neutral matrix for inquiry.

Postmodernism in this sense is larger than poststructuralism. It encompasses not only Foucault, Derrida, and Lacan, but also such theorists as Habermas, Gramsci, Bakhtin, and Bourdieu, who provide alternative frameworks for conceptualizing signification. If we understand postmodernism as the imperative of theorizing from within the horizon of the linguistic turn, then we can view a large group of thinkers as offering different ways of doing just that, and we can assess their relative merits from a feminist perspective. If, however, we follow Judith Butler and Drucilla Cornell in rejecting the term "postmodernism," we do more than simply protest reductive polemics that conflate different views; we also risk balkanizing the theoretical field—segregating various camps from one another, refusing to entertain questions posed from other perspectives, and foreclosing debate concerning the full range of options. But, of course, such debate can be foreclosed just as well by tendentious, sectarian definitions of postmodernism. If we follow Seyla Benhabib in associating that term with the aestheticization of historical inquiry and the rejection of universalist norms, we risk dismissing out of hand some ways of taking language seriously that are potentially useful for feminist theorizing.

The trick, once again, is to avoid false antitheses. From within the field of what are too often presented as mutually incompatible alternatives, we need to distinguish those elements that can be recontextualized and fruitfully articulated with one another in a feminist problematic from those that are genuinely inassimilable or otherwise untenable.

To that end, I want to recast some of the disagreements between Benhabib, Butler, Cornell, and myself precisely as disputes over the most fruitful way for feminists of making the linguistic turn. Roughly speaking, we are presented here with three pure, let us say "party-line," alternatives: 1) a Habermassian perspective oriented to the validity claims implicit in intersubjective communication, which are held to ground a discourse ethics and a procedural conception of democratic publicity (Benhabib); 2) a Foucauldian perspective oriented to a plurality of contingent, historically specific, power-laden discursive regimes that construct various subject positions from which innovation is possible (Butler); and 3) a Lacanian/Derridean perspective oriented to a masculine, phallogocentric symbolic order that suppresses the feminine while dissimulating its own groundlessness (Cornell).

Which of these three approaches should feminists embrace? Rather than opt for any one of them in its pure form, I propose that we try instead to develop a fourth alternative: an impure, eclectic, neopragmatist approach that combines the strongest features of all three. This fourth approach would encompass the full range of processes by which the sociocultural meanings of gender are constructed and contested. It would maximize our ability to contest the current gender hegemony and to build a feminist counterhegemony.

Such an eclectic, neopragmatist approach is advisable, I think, given the range and complexity of the phenomena we need to theorize. Gender dominance is socially pervasive, after all, imbricated in political economy and in political culture, in state apparatuses and in public spheres. Gender power traverses households, kinship networks, and the gamut of institutions comprising civil society. It operates at all sites of cultural and ideological production, including mass cultures, high cultures, academic cultures, oppositional cultures and countercultures. Gender struggle pervades everyday life, inflecting sexuality, reproduction, desire, taste, and habitus. It infuses personal identities and collective identities, social affinities and social antagonisms, and more-or-less shared common sense.

Every arena and level of social life is shot through with gender hierarchy and gender struggle. Each therefore requires feminist theorization. Each, however, is also traversed by other, intersecting axes of stratification and power, including class, "race"/ethnicity, sexuality, nationality, and age—a fact that vastly complicates the feminist project. Although gender dominance is ubiquitous, in sum, it takes different forms at different junctures and sites, and its character varies for differently situated women. Its shape cannot be read off from one site or one group and extrapolated to all the rest.

Thus, the task facing feminists is formidable. If we are to have any hope of understanding just what it is that we are up against, we need an approach that is simultaneously supple and powerful. We need frameworks that are sensitive to specificity, but that nevertheless permit us to grasp very large objects of inquiry, such as the global economy. We also need approaches that promote our ability to think relationally and contextually, including frameworks that can connect various elements of the social totality, casting those elements not merely as "different" from one another but as mutually interconnected. In addition, we need approaches that allow us to posit big summary accounts of the overall historical trajectory of gender power and gender struggle. These will necessarily be simplifying, to be sure; but if treated fallibilistically they can provide provisional orientation, a revisable sense of where we are heading and where we want to go. We need, finally, theoretical frameworks that permit us to project utopian hopes, envision emancipatory alternatives, and infuse all of our work with a normative critique of domination and injustice.

Where, then, does language fit in? Every aspect of gender hierarchy and gender struggle has an irreducible signifying dimension. Every arena of social life is infused with signifying practices, and every action is undertaken from within a horizon of cultural meanings and interpretations. The signifying dimension is as central to the systematic rape of Bosnian women and to the superexploitation of female factory operatives in the maquilladora region of Mexico as it is to the reception of Madonna and to MTV. It cannot be restricted to a specific sphere or realm, such as "culture" or "the lifeworld." It traverses the entire social field.

Much feminist work, therefore, consists in analyzing how cultural meanings of gender are produced and circulated. Such analysis, however, needs to be socially and historically contextualized, situated in time and place, institutionally and structurally grounded. It also needs to be linked to other modes of critical theorizing. Although signification is everywhere, it remains one dimension of sociality among others. One of the most important—and most difficult—tasks for feminist theorizing is to connect discursive analyses of gender significations with structural analyses of institutions and political economy.

How, then, should feminist theorists proceed? Given the complexity of our task, it is doubtful that any single approach to discourse or language will suffice. Certainly, none of the three pure approaches represented in this exchange can handle the full job by itself. Let us consider them one by one.

Benhabib's quasi-Habermassian approach offers some indispensable resources. She cogently defends the general feminist need for normative critique, emancipation-oriented historiography, and action-theoretical attention to women's aspirations and deeds. And she conceptualizes linguistic phenomena accordingly. By thematizing the validity claims implicit in intersubjective communication, Benhabib not only puts ethical questions at the center of feminist concern but also implicitly casts women as social subjects able to speak and to act against domination. From the speech-act theoretical perspective, domination inheres in communicative silences and imbalances: in implicit validity claims never subjected to rational critique, in deliberations tainted by the marginalization of female interlocutors. The Habermassian framework also provides a normative yardstick for the critique of institutions: the ideal of a democratized public sphere, an institutionalized arena of public discourse where procedural norms of fairness and equality promote parity of participation in the giving of and asking for reasons.

This approach has much to offer to feminists. It brings the *procedural* dimension of discourse, and with it the *normative* dimension, into focus. By problematizing the fairness of communicative processes (turn-taking, distribution of chances to make proposals or raise objections, etc.), Benhabib gives us a nonessentializing way of posing normative questions about discursive practice. To the extent, in other words, that we can identify procedural inequities in specific situations of communicative interaction, we can debunk bogus validity claims that might otherwise escape scrutiny. In addition, the concept of the public sphere is proving useful for institutional analysis. It has inspired important new feminist work in democratic theory,[1] in historiography,[2] and in cultural critique.[3]

For all its merits, however, Benhabib's approach does not provide everything feminists need. By definition, a procedural orientation brackets the *contents* of discourse; thus it cannot help us clarify the concrete substance of gendered meanings, nor their historical genealogies, nor their contemporary effects. In addition, a focus on justification and validity marginalizes questions about motivation and desire; thus, it cannot help us understand why women sometimes cling to perspectives that disadvantage them, even after the latter have been rationally demystified. More generally, because it stresses issues of *participation* in deliberation, Benhabib's approach valorizes the active, constituting side of individuals' involvement in communicative practice, to the relative neglect of the passive, constitut*ed* side.

Categories that work well for some purposes, in sum, are not necessarily well-suited to others. Forms of critique not easily broached from within Benhabib's framework include accounts of how specific communicative constraints are concretely and differentially institutionalized; accounts tracing the development of complexes of meaning that are relatively enduring across different communicative situations and that function as shared background commonsense; and critiques that generate substantive new emancipatory significations. For approaches that facilitate these genres of critical theorizing, we must turn our sights elsewhere.

Judith Butler's quasi-Foucauldian framework is a good place to start looking. Butler cogently defends the need for denaturalizing critique, critique that reveals the contingent, performatively constructed character of what passes for necessary and unalterable. And she construes discursive phenomena in ways that facilitate such critique. By thematizing the performative dimension of signification, she spotlights the *act* in the speech act, or, in Sartrean parlance, the praxis in the practico-inert. From Butler's perspective, power inheres in the naturalization and reification of contingent, actively fabricated discursive contents, especially those constitutive of gendered identities. Domination is effectively contested, in her view, when what was held to be a simple reflection of the way things are is shown to be a performative construction. Not only does such critique delegitimate received significations, it also opens space for the production of alternatives. The latter do not emerge *ex nihilo*, however, but through what Butler calls *resignification*, acts of iteration that are also innovations.[4] Paradoxically, these acts are performed from, and indeed enabled by, subject positions that are themselves constructed by the very discursive regimes they contest.

Butler's approach, too, has much to offer to feminists. It brings into focus the *performative* dimension of signification, hence the latter's inherent *historicity* and susceptibility to change. By figuring discursive change as resignification, moreover, Butler posits a linguistic subject that is nontranscendental yet capable of innovation. She understands that subject positionally, too, speaking as she does of a plurality of *subject positions*, each of which is correlated with some *discursive regime*. As a result, Butler's approach lets us grasp the concrete interplay of constraint and maneuver in specific discursive settings. It has already proved useful for feminist cultural critique—not only in traditional performance contexts, such as theatre and dance, but also in the wider terrain of gendered performance in everyday life. Butler's stress on dereification, lastly, valorizes *genealogy* as a mode of feminist critique. This, too, has yielded some good results. By uncovering the contingent historical origins of apparently natural commonsense notions, such as "female dependency",[5] feminist genealogists have contested the masculinism of mainstream political culture.

Yet Butler's approach does not give us all we need. Its internal normative resources—reification of performativity is bad, dereification is good—are far too meager for feminist purposes.[6] Genealogy requires a more robust ethical basis to achieve its emancipatory effects, as do other genres of critique that are equally necessary to feminism. Revealingly, Butler's own applications of her approach presuppose strong normative commitments; a moral objection to "exclusion" runs consistently through *Bodies That Matter*,[7] and anti-racism informs her essay[8] on the May 1992 acquittal of the police officers who assaulted Rodney King. Like Foucault, however, Butler has explicitly renounced the moral-theoretical resources necessary to aaccount for her own implicit normative judgments. But perhaps her views on this point are changing, as she has recently begun to appeal to "radical democracy."[9] Although so far this appeal remains a rhetorical gesture, as opposed to a conceptually developed commitment, I read it as an acknowledgment that feminist politics requires a more comprehensive moral-political vision than mere dereification of performativity.

In its present form, however, Butler's framework privileges the local, the discrete, and the specific. It is consequently not well suited to the crucial work of articulation, contextualization, and provisional totalization. It does not, for example, help us to map the links among various discrete discursive regimes and thus to theorize the construction of hegemony. Nor does it help us to contextualize—and thereby to realistically assess—the seemingly expansive, gender-bending performative possibilities of everyday life in relation to structural dynamics involving large-scale institutions, such as states and economies. Hence, in *Gender Trouble*, Butler vastly overestimated the emancipatory potential of such gender-bending performance in everyday life. She missed its susceptibility to commodification, recuperation, and depoliticization—especially in the absence of strong social movements struggling for social justice. (For a more balanced and sober assessment of gender-bending, see the film *Paris Is Burning*, which captures both the aspirations for transcendence in, and the limitations of, transvestite ball culture among poor gay men of color in New York.)

In addition, Butler's framework does not help us to theorize the relation of embodied individuals, with their relatively enduring dispositions (habitus), to the dispersed subject positions they successively occupy. Nor are we given a means to theorize intersubjectivity, the relations to one another of such individuals. Part of the difficulty here stems from Butler's tendency, when discussing subjectivity, to shift too quickly and without adequate differentiation among various conceptual levels—from, for example, the structural-linguistic level (at which she invokes a quasi-Saussurean account of the function of the shifter "I") to the psychoanalytic level (at which she invokes a quasi-Kristevan account of the *intra*psychic process of individual, ontogenetic subject-formation via abjection) to the institutional level (at which she invokes a quasi-Foucauldian account of the constitution of various different and distinct *subject-positions* at various different and distinct institutional sites) to the level of collective identifications (at which she invokes a quasi-Žižekian account of the phantasmatic and exclusionary character of politicized collective identities such as "women"). Failing as she does to distinguish these levels, Butler never considers the important and difficult problem of how to theorize their relations to one another.[10] Thus, she does not help us conceptualize the social totality.

In sum, Butler's approach is good for theorizing the micro level, the intrasubjective, and the historicity of gender relations. It is not useful, in contrast, for the macro level, the intersubjective, and the normative. For approaches that can help us get at those crucial aspects of gender relations, we must look somewhere else.

Significantly, although neither Benhabib nor Butler provides everything we need, their approaches are in many ways complementary. Benhabib supplies several resources that are underdeveloped in Butler: access to the intersubjective dimension of discourse, an orientation to the social totality, and some resources for normative critique. Butler, conversely, provides some of what is wanting in Benhabib: a nuanced view of the *intra*subjective interplay between creativity and constraint, an orientation to micro-level detail and historical specificity, and some resources for denaturalizing critique. Each, in other words, could help remedy the lacunae of the other—provided we could find some way of jettisoning their respective sectarian metaphysics and of combining their respective strengths.

Enter Drucilla Cornell. Her quasi-Lacanian/Derridean framework aims to integrate the best of Butler and Benhabib. Like Butler, Cornell defends the project of denaturalizing critique, especially critique that reveals that the purportedly fixed and simply given view of the feminine as "lack" is actually a cultural construction. Like Benhabib, however, Cornell also defends ethical and utopian thinking, especially thinking that projects emancipatory new significations of "the feminine within sexual difference." In general, then, Cornell wants to have it both ways. By linking denaturalizing critique with ethical-utopian thought, she aims to develop a genre of feminist theorizing that can challenge gender hierarchy without capitulating to androcentrism.

Cornell's aims are well worth pursuing. The project of linking denaturalizing critique, normative ethical critique, and utopian thinking is immensely attractive. So is the political goal of challenging both androcentrism and gender hierarchy simultaneously. I do not believe, however, that the theoretical framework Cornell proposes can actually help us achieve these goals.

Consider Cornell's conception of signification. She follows Lacan in postulating that "the structures of conscious language are genderized through an unconscious erasure of the feminine from the symbolic order, inseparable from the erasure of the significance of the

Mother [which] takes place through the erection of the phallus as the transcendental signifier . . ." (this volume p. 150). Presupposed here is a conception of language that is theoretically dubious and politically disabling. Cornell assumes a single masculine "phallogocentric symbolic order" that is culturally and discursively pervasive. This assumption is overtotalizing, however. It misleadingly posits unity and coherence among what are actually a diverse plurality of discursive regimes, subject positions, signifying practices, public spheres, and significations—including divergent and conflicting significations of femininity, which are surely not all reducible to "lack." As a result, Cornell's view of language effectively erases conflicts of interpretation, discursive struggles, and the differential positioning of different women, all of which are crucial to feminist theory. In addition, her framework erases history. Although she professes an interest in historicity, temporality, and emancipatory historiography, Cornell grounds her posit of a phallogocentric symbolic order in an ahistorical account of the psychodynamics of individuation. Contrary to her own best historicizing intentions, then, she makes historical shifts in cultural significations inconceivable.[11]

Cornell herself is uncomfortable with these implications. So she calls upon Derrida to rescue her from the Lacanian prisonhouse. Derrida, in her view, theorizes "what shifts" in language. He thus provides her with a set of metaphysical guarantees: that the linguistic code cannot be frozen, that the designation of the feminine as lack cannot be definitively stabilized, that the current structures of gender identity can never be adequate to the lived ambiguity of sexuality, and that their resymbolization is possible.

The Derridean guarantee is not precisely what is needed, however. "What shifts" is posited as a transcendental property of language operating beneath the apparently stable overarching symbolic order. It is an abstract promise that the latter could be otherwise. It is not a conception that can theorize actually existing cultural contestation among competing significations that are on a par with one another.[12] The result, unfortunately, is a tendency to devalue existing struggles as superficial and to privilege the Great Refusal. For if all of conscious language is phallogocentrically genderized, then the only acceptable alternative is the "Wholly Other." Cornell accordingly calls for the creation of an entirely new "feminine symbolic which feeds off the feminine imaginary." That, however, is politically tricky. To the extent that it manages to acquire any determinate content, it courts the sort of homogenizing essentialism that has proved so destructive of cross-class and cross-ethnic solidarity among women. And even in its abstract, indeterminate form, Cornell's call to resymbolize "the feminine within sexual difference" entrenches a conceptually and politically dubious gender binarism.

Cornell's framework, in sum, is fraught with theoretical and political difficulties. While I applaud her aim of marrying denaturalizing critique to ethical-utopian critique, I find her conception of language problematic. It effectively erases historicity, institutional specificity, situated normativity, and cultural contestation. Rather than retain some of its core theoretical elements, therefore, I prefer to detach Cornell's substantive insights about gender, sexuality, and the law from their current metaphysical underpinnings and to resituate them in a framework that is less totalizing, less essentializing, more historicized, and more institutionally grounded.

Where, then, does that leave our three pure alternatives? None of the three gives us everything that we need. Yet both Butler and Benhabib offer conceptions of discursive practice that can do important feminist critical work, while Cornell provides some profound insights into the ambiguous character of sexuality and some useful legal conceptions.[13]

If each of the three pure approaches has some but not all of what we need, then a fourth, impure alternative is called for. We need to cultivate the eclectic spirit I have invoked under the rubric of neopragmatism. This means adopting theoretical conceptions that permit both dereifying critique and normative critique, as well as the generation of new emancipatory significations. These conceptions should also enable us to articulate discourse analysis and political economy; studies of public spheres and of state apparatuses; genealogies of historians' categories and accounts of contestation "from below." Most importantly, they should allow us to theorize the intersection of gender, "race"/ethnicity, sexuality, nationality, and class *in every sociocultural arena*.

The key is to avoid metaphysical entanglements. We should adopt the pragmatic view that there are a plurality of different angles from which sociocultural phenomena can be understood. Which is best will depend on one's purposes. Feminist theorists share the general purpose of opposing male dominance, but we have many different more specific purposes. The latter vary with the intellectual task at hand and with the institutional and political contexts in which we work. As we take up different tasks in different contexts, we need to be able up to take up and discard different theoretical tools. We also need to allow for our mutual differences. This requires that we practice genealogy, for example, in a way that does not assume the sort of ontological commitments that would preclude normative critique of procedural inequities in public spheres. It also requires that we do normative critique and history from below so as not to preclude genealogy.[14] In general, conceptions of discourse, like conceptions of subjectivity, should be treated as tools, not as the property of warring metaphysical sects.

Such a pragmatist approach by no means entails capitulation to positivism, as Drucilla Cornell has insinuated. It is premised, rather, as already noted, on the view that social phenomena contain an irreducible signifying dimension and cannot be understood objectivistically.[15] But a pragmatist approach makes explicit what we have already seen: discursive phenomena may be fruitfully approached from several different angles, depending on one's situation and aims.

Nor is it the case, as Seyla Benhabib has alleged, that such a pragmatist approach is Pollyanna-ish. It is grounded, rather, on a sober appreciation of the magnitude of the tasks we face as feminists and of the insufficiency of any pure approach taken alone. I have never suggested, moreover, that fashioning some new synthesis will be easy. My first contribution to this volume argued that it was possible in principle to split some of the differences between Butler and Benhabib by, for example, fashioning new understandings of subjectivity. Faced with an unnecessarily polarized debate, I sought to safeguard the conceptual space within which such theoretical work could be done and to indicate some parameters of the problem. I did not intend to minimize the difficulties.

Here, too, I have sought to distinguish false antitheses from genuine contradictions. I have suggested, yet again, that aspects of Habermassian feminism can be coherently combined with aspects of Foucauldian feminism. But I have not claimed that any and every theory will do. On the contrary, I have argued that core features of at least one version of Lacanian/Derridean feminism should not be accommodated in the mix. For they work against some decisive feminist purposes.

It remains to be seen, of course, precisely how an eclectic, neopragmatist feminist theory will develop. That it *should* develop—and indeed *is* developing—seems clear. But its concrete elaboration is a collective task for a political and intellectual movement.

Notes

1. Seyla Benhabib, "Models of Public Space: Hannah Arendt, the Liberal Tradition, and Jürgen Habermas," and Nancy Fraser, "Rethinking the Public Sphere: A Contribution to the Critique of Actually Existing Democracy," both in *Habermas and the Public Sphere*, ed. Craig Calhoun (The M.I.T. Press, 1991).

2. Joan B. Landes, *Women and the Public Sphere in the Age of the French Revolution* (Cornell University Press, 1988); Mary P. Ryan, *Women in Public: Between Banners and Ballots, 1825–1880* (The Johns Hopkins University Press, 1990) and "Gender and Public Access: Women's Politics in Nineteenth Century America," in *Habermas and the Public Sphere*, ed. Craig Calhoun, op. cit.; and Evelyn Brooks Higginbotham, *Righteous Discontent: The Women's Movement in the Black Baptist Church, 1880–1920* (Harvard University Press, 1993).

3. Rita Felski, *Beyond Feminist Aesthetics* (Harvard University Press, 1989); Nancy Fraser, "Sex, Lies, and the Public Sphere: Some Reflections on the Confirmation of Clarence Thomas," *Critical Inquiry* vol 18 (1992), pp. 595–612; Nancy Fraser, "Clintonism, Welfare, and the Antisocial Wage: The Emergence of a Neoliberal Political Imaginary," *Rethinking Marxism* vol 6, no. 1 (1993), pp. 9–23; and Miriam Hansen, *Babel and Babylon: Spectatorship in American Silent Film* (Harvard University Press, 1991).

4. Butler's view here bears a striking resemblance to that of Julia Kristeva, as articulated in her early (1973) essay, "The System and the Speaking Subject," in *The Kristeva Reader*, ed. Toril Moi (Columbia University Press, 1986). For a critical account of the strengths and weaknesses of Kristeva's early view (and of its subsequent degeneration into a Lacanian-influenced neo-structuralist gender determinism) see Nancy Fraser, "The Uses and Abuses of French Discourse Theories for Feminist Politics," in *Revaluing French Feminism: Critical Essays on Difference, Agency, and Culture*, ed. Nancy Fraser and Sandra Bartky (Indiana University Press, 1992).

5. Nancy Fraser and Linda Gordon, "A Genealogy of 'Dependency': Tracing a Keyword of the U.S. Welfare State," *Signs: Journal of Women in Culture and Society* vol. 19, no 2 (1994), pp. 309–336.

6. Butler incidentally misunderstands—or perhaps I should say, misreads—some of my previous criticisms of her views. First, in raising the issue of esotericism I was not suggesting that the use of difficult theoretical language is never justified; I was merely questioning whether *her* use of anti-humanist language was, i.e., whether it provided theoretical clarity and/or political gains. My doubts on this point have increased, moreover, in the light of her response to Benhabib. Chastizing Benhabib for taking her anti-humanist rhetoric at face value, Butler now stresses that she is actually trying to explain how agency is possible given the constitution of subjects by power regimes. For this purpose, however, an anti-humanist rhetoric seems counterproductive. Second, it is not the case that I (or Habermas, for that matter) hold that "ordinary language cannot provide ultimate grounds for adjudicating the validity of its own claims." Neither I nor Habermas is interested in "ultimate grounds"; and we both assume that the communicative practice of adjudicating validity claims transpires precisely in ordinary language, for no metalanguage exists. Lastly, Butler misunderstands my point about the political implications of foundationalist theories of subjectivity. I did not claim that Toussaint subversively cited an otherwise politically insidious Jacobin view and thereby redeemed it for progressive politics. I said, rather, that, like Toussaint, the Jacobins themselves put a foundationalist view to emancipatory uses—an assessment I share with Toussaint. My point in any event bears restating: one cannot deduce a single univocal political valence from a theory of subjectivity in the abstract, as Butler tried to do throughout her original essay. Nor, I might add, can one deduce anything from the difference (if there be any) between citing a previously extant signification and originating a new one. In any case, there have surely been "politically insidious" as well as progressive citations. So the problem of normative judgment remains.

7. Judith Butler, *Bodies That Matter: On the Discursive Limits of "Sex"* (New York: Routledge, 1993).

8. Judith Butler, "Endangered/Endangering: Schematic Racism and White Paranoia," in *Reading Rodney King, Reading Urban Uprising*, ed. Robert Gooding-Williams (New York: Routledge, 1993).

9. Judith Butler, *Bodies That Matter: On the Discursive Limits of "Sex,"* op. cit.

10. This conflation of levels is apparent in Butler's response to my previous criticisms. She claims, on the one hand, that I was mistaken in attributing to her a concern with the question "who is authorized to speak, and who is de-authorized into silence" (this volume p. 139)—despite my verbatim citation from her first essay of a passage about "deauthorized subjects, pre-subjects, figures of abjection, populations erased from view" (this volume p. 47). She claims that her primary interest, rather, is the "exclusionary formation of the subject" understood as a constitutive *intra*psychic operation, not an *inter*subjective process or relation. Yet she also claims this "psychoanalytic premise . . . might [be] usefully employ[ed] in the service of a political critique." To explain how the premise might be so employed, however, she reverts to the example of masculinist figures of mastery, which "have required the de-subjectivation of the feminine," and she then goes on to endorse my questions about *intersubjective* equity: "can we overcome or at least ameliorate the asymmetries in current practices of subjectivation?" (this volume p. 139). In general, then, Butler oscillates between intrasubjective and intersubjective claims, and between claims that she is and is not interested in intersubjectivity. As I see it, her framework is still primarily anchored in a philosophy of subjectivity, albeit in the mode of a reversal or abstract negation. As such, it has difficulty dealing with issues involving intersubjectivity, including the justice of relations among subjects. Yet Butler does (sometimes) want to deal with such issues. And she seems to appreciate that her claim to political relevance ultimately depends on the ability of her framework to connect up with and to illuminate such matters. Hence her oscillation between *intra*subjective and *inter*subjective claims.

11. For an extended argument, see Nancy Fraser, "The Uses and Abuses of French Discourse Theories for Feminist Politics," op. cit. and my "Introduction" to *Revaluing French Feminism*, op. cit.

12. For further arguments, see Nancy Fraser, "The Force of Law: Metaphysical or Political?" *Cardozo Law Review* vol. 13, no. 4 (1991) pp. 1325–1331. Cornell's response seems to me to misunderstand this point. Claiming (mistakenly) that I have accused her of foundationalism, she replies that by stressing "the impossibility of Woman," she "opens up endless possibilities for the re-elaboration of sexual difference" (this volume p. 147). This response, however, merely reasserts her good intentions of accommodating diversity and historicity. It does not show that they can in fact be realized within her conceptual framework. I remain convinced that they cannot. Cornell starts with the exorbitant and misleading hypothesis of a single, overarching, universal, ahistorical phallogocentric symbolic order. She then tries to introduce the possibility of change by positing an equally universal,

ahistorical property of language. The latter is too little, too late. A better approach would begin with the actual historical diversity of significatory phenomena, including the intense contemporary contestation surrounding the meanings of femininity, masculinity, sexuality, and sexual difference. And it would theorize the processes by which androcentric cultural hegemonies were (and are) both constructed and resisted from that diversity.

13. See, for example, Drucilla Cornell, "Gender, Sex, and Equivalent Rights," in *Feminists Theorize the Political,* ed. Judith Butler and Joan W. Scott (New York: Routledge, 1992).

14. I mean here to reject the Joan Scott-versus-Linda Gordon opposition as another false antithesis. Both of these historians have done extremely important work, but neither strikes me as the best judge of the other's merits, nor of the philosophical issues that divide them. For my views on Scott, see Nancy Fraser, "Review of Linda Nicholson, *Gender and History* and Joan W. Scott, *Gender and the Politics of History," NWSA Journal* vol 2, no. 3 (1990), pp. 505–508. For my own attempts at a genealogy that avoids disabling metaphysical entanglements, in a paper co-authored with Gordon, see Nancy Fraser and Linda Gordon, "A Genealogy of 'Dependency'," op. cit.

15. The main polemical thrust of my work on need interpretation, the public sphere, and the discursive construction of "welfare" and "dependency" is to oppose mainstream positivistic social science, which objectifies the discursive dimension. See, for example, Nancy Fraser, *Unruly Practices: Power, Discourse, and Gender in Contemporary Social Theory* (University of Minnesota Press, 1989); "Rethinking the Public Sphere," op. cit.; "Clintonism, Welfare, and the Antisocial Wage," op. cit.; and "A Genealogy of 'Dependency'," op. cit.

Index